This book introduces the Muslim-American community's guiding Islamic principle of citizenship responsibility. It is an intriguing part history of the development of Islam in America and the Muslim-American identity, part analysis of the crisis in Islamic world leadership, and part manifesto arguing the value of America's indigenous Muslim community in aiding the American public and leadership to effectively confront and abate the complex issue of Muslim extremism.

Earl Abdulmalik Mohammed combines authentic scholarship with common language in identifying specific Islamic principles which manifest for Muslim-Americans as both a social establishment philosophy of civic virtue, and a rooted, organic shelter protecting against extremism, while chiding American leadership for overlooking and under-appreciating what is its most valuable, native and exportable ideological resource to nullify the threat of Muslim extremist influences.

This book is compulsory reading for anyone interested in clear recognition of what Islam is, what it is committed to, and how an American community of Muslims interprets it to champion democratic ideals and to defend the notion of a free, just, and productive society.

The believer is one whose neighbor is free from his harmful conduct.

~Muhammed the Prophet

Democracy, Civic Virtue, and Islam

*The Muslim-American Jihad
against Extremism*

"*In the Law of Settlements, there is the preservation of Life…*"
(Holy Qur'an 2:179)

EARL ABDULMALIK MOHAMMED

ISBN 978-1-4958-0953-8 Paperback
ISBN 978-1-4958-0954-5 Hardback

Published May 2016

INFINITY PUBLISHING
1094 New DeHaven Street, Suite 100
West Conshohocken, PA 19428-2713
Toll-free (877) BUY BOOK
Local Phone (610) 941-9999
Fax (610) 941-9959
Info@buybooksontheweb.com
www.buybooksontheweb.com

"*If you say you are an American citizen, and other American citizens take you to be an enemy, then your citizenship is in trouble. Our citizenship must be meaningful. It must be of value to us and our fellow citizens.*"

-W. Deen Mohammed

About the Cover: Authentic Islamic teachings appropriate the influence of colors and their use in symbolic forms and imagery as a salute to Nature in its God-given role to inspire, educate, and refine human thinking and behavior. The choice for this book's cover art and design intends to obey such Islamic teachings. It is also intended, by the use of specific colors and symbols and the Muslim-American and American flags, to make a necessary commentary on their misappropriation by misanthropic ideologies in today's world as well as underscoring the vital concerns shared by democracies and Islamic communities worldwide.

"Do you not see that Allah sends down rain from the sky? With it We then bring forth vegetation of various colors. And in the mountains are white and red areas of various shades of color and intense black in hue. And so it is among human beings and crawling creatures and cattle that they are of various colors. Among His worshippers those who have knowledge are they who properly regard Allah."

-Holy Qur'an 35:27-28

For each of my children:

We are forced to be apart, but I am comforted by thoughts of you. Your face. Your eyes. Your hands. Your feet. Your mind. Your heart. I see you. I know you. I believe in you.

Our life must move forward. The life we talk about. The life we laugh about. The life we cry over. The life we dream of. The life we are created for. Our human life. We have taught you to embrace that life. To tighten your grip on the struggle and difficulty of the moment with innocence, dignity, faith, knowledge, courage, confidence, strength of will, strength of character, and strength of determination — but without arrogance or ignorance. The world cannot live honorably without that life. You are a new breath for the world. A new birth.

I pray to Allah, the Most High:

That Principles, which promote Trust between citizens and their governments, are appreciated more and practiced more. That Peace is the immediate and lasting objective of nations and leaders. That Muslim-Americans will abide by their finest teachings, and continue to join all people of conscience in a commitment to preserve justice and goodwill. That you will be all Allah created you to be, and that America's social order will respect and promote that without selfish or unnecessary impediments. And if America sustains that, or if She loses her way, that you will stand prepared, as an example, to help Her.

My daughters and sons, this book is for you, and your children – our life moving forward.

With love,
Daddy

About the Author

Earl Abdulmalik Mohammed has been a distinguished spokesman for Islam and Muslim affairs for a quarter century. He is a lifelong student of Islamic knowledge, and an accomplished instructor of religion and scriptural sciences. He has earned advanced credits in international and Arabic language studies from the Middle East Institute, Georgetown University, and the Modern Arabic Language Institute of Yemen in Sana'a. He served for fifteen years as the National Representative for Imam W. Deen Mohammed and his Ministry, the late leader of the largest Muslim community in the Western hemisphere. In that capacity he addressed congregations at mosques, churches, and synagogues, made presentations to government representatives and bodies, participated in formal discussions with political, cultural, and social leaders and organizations, and lectured at dozens of colleges and universities throughout North America. On behalf of Imam W. Deen Mohammed and the Muslim-American community he traveled to meet with leaders in Africa, Europe, the Middle East, and Asia, and participated in conferences and programs in Saudi Arabia, Malaysia, Ethiopia, and Italy, among other countries. He has been interviewed by major print and electronic media, and written several articles on Islam in America including an "Open Letter to all Americans" that appeared in USA Today shortly after the September 11 attacks.

When Imam W. Deen Mohammed announced his resignation as leader in the society of Muslim-Americans some major U.S. newspapers speculated Earl Abdulmalik Mohammed to be his logical successor ("Influential Leader Steps Down," *The Los Angeles Times,* September 13, 2003; "A Journey of Faith," *The Baltimore Sun,* August 16, 1998). In December 2001 at a public forum in Grand Rapids, Michigan Imam Mohammed was asked if there were any persons from his community who could represent Islam and Muslims the way he did. He said in response, "Earl Abdulmalik Mohammed, in my opinion, is responsible for most of the propagating of the true image of Muslims in America. Not just for us, but for all Muslims (*The Muslim Journal Newspaper,* December 14, 2001)."

In 2013 Earl Abdulmalik Mohammed was convicted of a single count of mail fraud related to his family business. He is currently serving a U.S. federal prison sentence.

With *Democracy, Civic Virtue, and Islam: The Muslim-American Jihad Against Extremism,* his enlightened advocacy of Muslim-American interests and representation of Islam in its true image continues.

Acknowledgements

We thank Allah, the Merciful Benefactor, the Merciful Redeemer, the Mighty and Sublime. Highly Glorified is He. Lord-Cherisher-Sustainer-Guardian-Evolver of all the systems of knowledge. Guarantor of Faith and all sacred Trusts. Owner of all that exists. Author of Religion and its laws, Pardoner of sins. No vision can grasp Him, yet He is ever-watching over all. He is not created but is Creator of everything. Originator of Nature, Revealer of Guidance, Dispatcher of Prophets and Messengers, Bestower of every kindness on His creation. We praise Him, The Preserver and Increaser of all favors, Hearer and Grantor of our prayers. We witness that He, alone, deserves our worship and that nothing is partner with Him in the Rule of all He has created. We witness that Muhammed is His Messenger, the perfected and completed human being, to whom the Book of Guidance with no defects, the Qur'an, was revealed and entrusted. He is our guide, and a mercy to all creation. We pray that Allah's choicest blessings be upon him, and the peace. Amen.

I am indebted to many people, but none above my parents and my family. May Allah preserve and protect them all.

To those individuals who understood the importance of this work and had confidence in my ability to complete it, I am grateful.

To those very special ones who offered their prayers, unconditional love, support, labor, and tears, and without whose sacrifices and efforts this work would not have been completed. May Allah reward you greatly.

In memory of our late leader, the Reformer in these times, the Imam of Al-Islam, and Leader of a People, W. Deen Mohammed, his instruction and example continue to inspire and lead us. May Allah grant him Mercy.

Allah is all good and accepts only good. We trust Him for all good results.

Foreword

In the late eighties, the late leader of Muslim-Americans, Imam W. Deen Mohammed (d. 2008), delivered a public address in Dallas, Texas entitled, "You Have to be Prepared to Make It in the Land of Plenty." In that speech he quoted a selection from a booklet published and distributed by an organization called the World Association of Muslim Youth (WAMY) headquartered in Riyadh, Saudi Arabia. That selection read, "Christians and Jews are Disbelievers and Should be Killed."

Imam Mohammed summarily condemned the statement and the publication as "bullshit literature," and sternly warned the publishing organization that any and all literature conveying the same or similar sentiments introduced into the United States would be openly discredited and exposed as an example of what and who Islam and the Muslim-American community rejects as un-Islamic. He apologized to the audience— which consisted of persons of different faiths—and explained that he believed that publications like those were purposely distributed in the United States to weaken the determination of his community to build and maintain friendships and working relationships with other faith communities. He also made clear that he would personally and publicly oppose all attempts by any group of Muslims in the United States, or any Muslim nation, to influence the American public to believe that Islam and Muslims are only interested in making converts, and care nothing for the integrity of other faith traditions and their communities. Later, in the mid-nineties I was present at a meeting in Riyadh, Saudi Arabia at the WAMY headquarters, where Imam Mohammed made this identical point to the publisher of that pamphlet, directly and irrevocably.

A few months after the September 11 attack, I was in a private meeting with Imam Mohammed, where he recalled that occasion in Dallas. He pointed out to me in graphic terms that the Muslim-American community's biggest adversary was Muslim leadership from abroad who did not approve of him as successor to his father (Elijah Muhammad). He had been generally impervious to their 'offers' of religious guidance and financial support. He said to me that they had an ongoing plan to plant their most radical notions among unsuspecting African-American Muslims, but the effectiveness of his leadership and the loyalty of Muslim-Americans to him interfered. He said they had long thought of us as their 'fruit for harvest,' to be used in their schemes and according to their interests. He advised me – as he did many others over the years – of his expectations that they would continue that strategy in one form or another until they had a foothold of ideological influence and control over Islam and Muslims in America. From the earliest days of his leadership he had emphasized the primary importance of acquiring correct religious knowledge. This was always the highest priority. For him it was imperative that the community be able to use that knowledge as a defense against such corrupting influences, and to guard our autonomy. He sensitized me in that conversation more than ever of his conviction to promote Islam in a way as to highlight its teachings on how Muslims are to steward relationships and trust as citizens and as members in the universal brotherhood of all faiths.

Interestingly, during that meeting he gave me a revised description of my job as his National Representative. He said, "I want you to make friends for us with all people of goodwill."

He took time in that meeting to specifically explain the Qur'an's inherent protective devices — how they are found, understood, used, and what conditions trigger their activation and implementation. He concluded that meeting with a very serious directive: "Do you understand what I have given you now? Use it for the good of our people. Share it in 'your time' if you know of those who can appreciate it, or when you think it necessary and appropriate." Looking back at those few hours we spent at an IHOP restaurant on Chicago's south side nearly a decade and a half ago, it was as if he was administering a sacred oath to me. I am sure others had similar experiences with him.

I have not shared with any individual or group the details of that meeting, though I have reminisced about them often. Over the years I have thought deeply on what he personally expressed to me of his hopes and expectations for Islam and Islamic community life in America, and similarly reflected on and studied his inspired language of religious insight, understanding, and instruction; and his socio-religious thought and leadership methods. For the first time, I introduce what he taught me that day in this book, albeit in a summarized form. I also introduce here the Muslim-American philosophy of civic virtue and citizenship responsibility. Imam Mohammed referred to it as our 'principle of binding and engagement,' and taught it to me and others over the many years of his leadership.

Those who knew me then, and knew my relationship with him, know well that I understood him in a way others did not. He trusted my understanding of what he taught, and he promoted my ability to share that understanding with others. I believe he would have expected this book, strongly approved it, and distributed it with his own hands.

It is important to point out that I originally intended the basic content of this book as a letter of concern to our Muslim-American leaders and public leaders of our country. But, as I observed the spreading poison of extremism begin to choke our country's good senses and ability to reason responsibly in the national public discourse on the matter, I felt my letter would be insufficient. The increasing marginalization of the truth of Islamic ideas and the image of Islam is contributing to a public paranoia and creating a dangerous vacuum of bias. Due in large part to opinions molded and driven by incessant media coverage of war and horrific acts of violence perpetrated against innocents by extremist Muslims, I was finally compelled to expand that original letter into this publication.

With this book it is my hope to introduce the Muslim-American community and its essential leadership principle into the discussion of how the American public and leadership can better confront the complex issue of extremism. I have attempted to argue, with as much scholarly vigor as one can muster under my present circumstances, that the Muslim-American community associated with Imam W. Deen Mohammed has a central, strategic importance in defeating extremist influences in America and abroad. It is very disturbing to me that most Americans do not know this. To the extent that this fact remains under-appreciated and overlooked is a grave disservice to our fellow citizens and to a world searching for answers.

I commend this work to the people of understanding, to the learned, to the authorized, and for the benefit of the common person—the common, good citizens in all nations, states, and sovereignties. We Muslim-Americans have devoted our lives to the disciplines of Islamic faith and traditions for God's pleasure. We are building our institutions upon this devotion, and we are instructing our children in its sanctity. We look for ultimate approval from God. Yet, in this temporal existence we strive to earn recognition as a trusted community of contributors working for the best conditions for human life on this earth, as God intended. In this nation we want our leaders to not merely see us, but know us and respect us in our place alongside all other groups of noble conscience. We do not desire this for status. We desire it as a people—as citizens—within whose history, language of discovery and experiences, and perspective, are proofs of the value we place on the sacred life's freedoms and natural human rights identified by the Founders of the American Republic. Thus, we abide by God's words in our Holy Book: "In the Law of Settlements there is the Preservation of Life…;" we comprehend the responsibility illuminated in the Constitution to "secure the blessings of liberty…;" and we want to be trusted as other citizens are with our share of the duty. It is my prayer that this book makes the argument readily.

Earl Abdulmalik Mohammed
October 9, 2015
Butner, NC

Table of Contents

Introduction

Muslims in general, particularly of Western nations, who strive to live according to the teachings of Islam in its truest report and practice, are faced with daunting challenges today. While they assert that Islam is and wants 'peace,' that conviction can appear to ignore or avoid facts which suggest that a significant minority of Muslims are a global threat to civilized society. It is acknowledged that extremists operating in Syria, Iraq, Yemen, Nigeria, Afghanistan, Pakistan, and other polities, touting radical rhetoric and committing unconscionable crimes, are primarily responsible for that threat. These extremists have created prodigious security concerns for those states and seriously impaired their ability to protect and govern their populations. The implications of these facts are not lost on democratic Western states.

While Western authorities struggle daily in deciding how best to support their counterparts and allies where the extremists operate overtly and from numerous safe havens, of greater long-term importance is addressing the extremists's potential reach and threat at home. All Western democratic governments have identified domestic threat assessment and counter-terrorism measures as top priorities. However, these democracies have been saddled with vociferous public debate over the 'security verses liberty' question.

Nevertheless, the development of strategies that effectively characterize and negate the extremists' nefarious influence on indigenous Western Muslim populations without stereotyping, coercing,[1] or otherwise compromising the rights of law-abiding, productive citizens is a necessary task. Perhaps surprisingly, assistance and precedent for structuring and supporting such strategies can be found within fundamental Islamic principles.[2] Muslim civilians who value their citizenship and have awareness of these teachings, or become acquainted with them, would be ideologically suited and materially prepared to support their government's efforts. It is intended that this book introduce those principles and serve as an aid in understanding how they can be applied.

Part I: Analysis

"If it were Our will, We could drown them: then there would be no help-er (to hear their cry), nor could they be saved; except by way of Mercy from Us, and worldly convenience (to serve them) for a time. When they are told, fear that which is before you and that which will be after you, in order that you may receive Mercy."

The Holy Qur'an 36:43-45

1   The Two Sacred Mosques

In introducing this discussion, a review of issues surrounding the Persian Gulf War, specifically Iraq's aggression against Saudi Arabia, is cited to place in perspective today's extremists' influence on Western Muslim populations. Particularly instructive, and aiding this book's inquiry into identifying Islamic teachings that support the development of tactics to neutralize and counter the present Muslim extremist threat within Western society, are facts revealing the role and value of Americans in the Saudi's overall preparation and response to Iraq's threats and 1991 invasion of the Kingdom.

As Operation Desert Shield transitioned to Operation Desert Storm, and the world watched stunned as the Iraqi army plundered Kuwait and threatened an incursion of Saudi Arabia, the rulers of the Kingdom and their advisory council of Islamic scholars invited a delegation of Muslim-Americans[3] there for urgent consultations. Those meetings preceded an international conference where Muslim officials, scholars, and leaders were to discuss an Islamic response to Iraq's aggression against Kuwait. However, attendees were well aware that the pressing Islamic question was the appropriateness and acceptability of inviting non-Muslim forces to defend the two most sacred sites in Islam: the Sacred Mosque at Makkah and the Prophet's Mosque at Madinah. What seemed an imminent Iraqi invasion of Saudi Arabia posited serious political, military, and socio-economic concerns, but also equally grave theological questions. All with global implications.

Though American-led allied forces would be stationed, by invitation, on sovereign soil and defending sovereign borders, it was reasoned that they would also be a de-facto defending force of the Sacred Precincts of Makkah and Madinah. That scenario raised two very serious issues: first, the defense of the Saudi nation, its people and its economic infrastructure; second, the protection of Islam's most sacred areas and the status of the Saudi royal family's special role in their maintenance and security.[4] The first issue was primarily a Saudi state concern. The second issue invited the legitimate interest of the entire Muslim world.

For many in the Muslim world, and the religious scholars from which they took instruction and guidance, the reality of a non-Muslim military force 'dug in' near the Haramain (the Two Inviolable Precincts) was a moral outrage. They reasoned that for any non-Muslim to be on the same soil as the 'Haramain,' where the religion of Islam pronounces its nativity and where daily tens of thousands (millions annually) of the Muslim faithful observe doctrinal religious rites all hours of the day and night,[5] was illegal and punishable under Islamic law. Masjid Al-Haram at Makkah (The Sacred House) and Masjid An-Nabi at Madinah (The Prophet's Mosque) are the center of Islamic worship, origin, and identity.[6] The rulers of Saudi Arabia were not only faced with an invading army and its threat to the safety of their people and the long term security and independence of their nation, but also with the response of the Islamic world to the possibility of having the holiest places of Islam come under the control of a rogue regime and its heretical ideology,[7] or have them defiled by the presence of foreign forces understood by many Muslims to be 'disbelievers'.

The relationship complexities between the Arab states have little to do with Islamic teachings or practices. Though Saddam Hussein was widely regarded in the Muslim and Arab world as a menace and loathed by the Saudi's leadership establishment, it was the perception that the Sacred Precincts were being "occupied" by non-Muslim forces that could potentially inflame the passions of literally hundreds of millions of Muslims worldwide. The Saudi leadership had long understood that its 'custodianship' of the Two Holy Mosques was tenuous; accepted begrudgingly in the Muslim world partly because of the political accommodation which created it.[8] In the context of the Saudi's immediate response to the invasion of Kuwait and Saddam's threats against the Kingdom, the convening of Islamic leaders was not an attempt to appear conciliatory to international Muslim sentiments. In the minds of most Muslims the defense of the Holy Precincts superseded issues of Saudi sovereignty. Therefore, under these circumstances, the convening of an international conference was not merely advisable. It was necessary.

For all of their wealth and economic influence, centuries of Islamic tradition, and claim to high Islamic civilization and knowledge, the Saudi leadership understood they were ill-prepared to deal with this enemy alone. From a political and military perspective, and in terms of defending economic interests, the assistance of the United States was universally understood. Even the leadership of Muslim nation-states whose relations with the Saudis was lukewarm, would not question the necessity of America's military involvement given the importance of shared Saudi-American economic concerns, their global importance, and the volatility and unpredictability of Saddam Hussein. After all, the Royal Kingdom of Saudi Arabia and the United States of America were open allies. Furthermore, no military force in the Arab world would reasonably expect to match the military readiness, might, and skill of an American force in a short term campaign. So, the insertion of the Americans from a Saudi national defense standpoint, or even as a remedy to secure a temporary but stable 'peace' in the region, could be tolerated. But the religious question was another matter entirely.

Even if there was no realistic expectation that Saddam's forces could penetrate far enough into the Kingdom to directly engage forces designated to defend Makkah or Madinah, the image of non-Muslims trampling the Holy Precincts had been firmly planted in the minds of Muslims everywhere. True or not, that image affected the security and stability of majority Muslim nations and Western nations with minority Muslim populations alike. The possibility of respected voices in the Islamic world morally decrying or legally condemning the Saudi royal family's inability to properly maintain the Haramain, as a rallying principle to hint at or justify deposing the Saudi regime and destroying its Islamic authority, was palpable. The moral, theological, and legal arguments against the Saudi rulers were essentially identical, i.e., if they could not provide their 'custodial' service without the assistance of non-Muslims, then they were not meeting their duty to God or their tacit contractual obligation to the international community of Muslims. This offense rendered them unfit as the 'Custodian(s) of the Two Holy Mosques,' and illegal claimants of such authority. The validity of the argument was debatable, but it was logical enough to incite and manipulate Muslim masses, and sufficiently serious for legitimate Islamic authorities to address it without delay.

The teachings of the Holy Qur'an are explicit concerning the importance of the House at Makkah, its physical and symbolic sanctity, as well as the lives of those that visit it. It also specifies the weighty responsibility of those trusted with its maintenance and security:

> *"The first House appointed for mankind was that at Bakkah,* full of blessing and of guidance for all created beings... whosoever enters it attains security."* (3:96-97) *another name for Makkah

> *"O you who believe, do not violate the sanctity of the Symbols of God... nor the people visiting the Sacred House."* (5:2)

> *"God made the Sacred House an asylum of security for all mankind...."* (5:97)

> *"Do you consider provisions to the pilgrims and the maintenance of the Sacred Mosque equal to the worth of those who believe in God...? They are not comparable...."* (9:19)

> *"No men can be its guardians except the God-fearing...."* (8:34)

> *"O you who believe, truly those who join others with the worship of God are corrupt, so let them not... approach the Sacred Mosque."* (9:28)

> *"The Sacred Mosque, which We have made open for mankind,-equal is the dweller there and the visitor. And any whose purpose there is corruption*

and wrongdoing then We will cause them to taste a severe penalty." (22:25)

Additionally, the authentic sayings of Prophet Muhammed, the prayers and peace be upon him,* to which the faithful and learned refer for explanation of the Qur'an and application of its teachings report that he said the following on the subject of the Holy Precincts of Makkah and Madinah: *a traditional salutation

> *"One prayer in my mosque (at Madinah) is better than a thousand prayers in any other mosque except for the Sacred Mosque (at Makkah)."* (from the Bukhari collection of hadith)

> *"Madinah is a protected sanctuary... its trees should not be cut, no evil words spoken nor any sin committed in it, and whoever (does these things) will incur the curse of God, the angels, and all of mankind."* (Bukhari)

> *"Madinah is a protected sanctuary... and a place of security to be secured by all of the Muslims, and whoever betrays a Muslim in this respect incurs the curse of God, the angels, and all of mankind."* (Bukhari)

> *"None plots against the people of Madinah but that he will be destroyed like the salt is dissolved in water."* (Bukhari)

> *"There will be no town in which the Dajjal (Great Deceiver) will not enter except Makkah and Madinah."* (Bukhari)

In addition to providing spiritual guidance these exhortations from the Qur'an and reported sayings of the Prophet are also legal pronouncements, codified, and enforceable under some interpretations of Islamic law. Concurrently, the Qur'an encourages the establishment of treaties and mutual agreements — any of which might stipulate cooperation for national defense — and vehemently condemns violation of them. The Prophet is known to have established such pacts with non-Muslims in the defense of Madinah, and in other matters, and strictly observed them.[9] Further, the Qur'an shames acts of naked aggression of any type.[10] From these perspectives, the Saudi rulers' invitation to whomever they needed to help defend and protect their national sovereignty against an aggressor was Islamically sound. However, these references did not necessarily support the Saudi plan for the protection of the Haramain.

Theoretically, if any respected scholar of Islam ruled that the American-led coalition was anything other than 'the God-fearing'[11] — which was likely — it was conceivable that Saddam's army of aggression could be joined or replaced, in time, by an international 'Islamic' force believing themselves to be liberators of the Two Sacred Mosques from a 'corrupt usurper and its protecting friends,'[12] or the enemy forces of the 'Great Deceiver'.[13] Likewise, any state with a significant Muslim population perceived as sympathetic or supportive of the Saudi cause could potentially risk open rebellion. Given these considerations it is not difficult to trace the line between this issue and the rise of extremist interpretations of Islam, particularly as it relates to the spike in organized terror attacks and membership in extremist groups in the twenty five years since then.[14]

Not since the time when international recognition of the modern Kingdom was still forming and the first king was actively consolidating and legitimizing his authority in the region,[15] had the Saudi ruling family feared their grip on power untenable. Under the circumstances of the Persian Gulf War, when the Saudi rulers wrestled with grave uncertainties concerning the survival of their nation and their authority over the two most sacred centers of Islamic faith, it is revealing that they called first upon American friendship and expertise for assistance; not only military and political, but also religious.

2   An Overlooked Role

"If it were Our will, We could drown them: then there would be no helper (to hear their cry), nor could they be saved; Except by way of Mercy from Us, and worldly convenience (to serve them) for a time. When they are told, fear that which is before you and that which will be after you, in order that you may receive Mercy."

The Holy Qur'an 36:43-45

Like all military operations, the Saudi rulers' plan for the defense of the Kingdom had short- and long-term ramifications; anticipated and unforeseen outcomes. With the plan's open and unabashed dependence on American military preparedness, a successful campaign to repel an Iraqi invasion was expected. The casualties — human, political, economic, or other, that would manifest as a result of the War — were not as predictable.

There was little doubt that speculations drawn from what the War revealed of the intricate inner workings of the Saudi-American alliance would intensify doubts in the Muslim world regarding the legitimacy of the Saudi's Islamic authority. But, the dominant concern for a swift and decisive end to the conflict was vitally more important to them than exposure of those arcane details. From the Saudi vantage point, if the Americans halted Saddam's march on the kingdom and neutralized his regional threat, they would have the security and time required to pursue another victory in the Islamic public relations war for their Muslim world credibility. Conversely, if the Americans were not a part of the defense equation, all could be lost: national sovereignty, capital interests, and their leadership roles in the Islamic world. Without American support, Saudi Arabia, as a state and institution of Islamic authority, could be completely destroyed.

At the behest of the senior Islamic scholars of the Kingdom,[16] counsel was sought from an unlikely scion of the American alliance: American Muslims, who by way of reports of their independent Islamic thinking, and unique socio-religious journey[17] had earned the respect and admiration of Muslim faithful and learned worldwide. Neither socialized nor educated as other leaders in the Muslim world, they had designated themselves Muslim-Americans,[18] and espoused an Islamic perspective firm in orthodox traditions of belief and practice, but fresh in understanding and application of them. Largely overlooked by observers of the dynamics of the War due to their lack of bold political or economic presence in America, their religious counsel would resonate in the Saudi leadership psyche as lastingly as the coalition's defense strategy.

Premised on a fundamental Islamic principle, the Muslim-American message to the Kingdom's rulers was uncomplicated and direct.[19] It was a reminder of Islam's high recognition of the idea of a just society:[20] In preparing to defend the Kingdom, the Saudi rulers were observing the duty that just governments owe their citizens.[21] By inviting Americans to aid in that defense they were also acknowledging Saudi-American common and vital interests, and thus, paying an invaluable public tribute to core values shared between two peoples abiding by their respective democratic ideals and religious teachings. Like democratic ideas of government,[22] Islam cherishes, and regards as a sacred matter, the inherent demand in every human being to be respected in society.[23] Islam interprets this demand as both an entitlement[24] and a natural endowment[25] that requisitions the respect, attention, and protection of all peoples and nations who value it.[26] Islam categorizes this recognition of the human individual and his societal destiny as the 'sacred property' of mankind,[27] and eternally enshrines its sanctity in the symbols of the Two Holy Mosques.[28] The act of guarding this 'sacred property' is further symbolized by duties ascribed to its 'custodian(s)'. For the King, as 'Custodian of the Two Holy Mosques', to act firmly and decisively where that 'property' or 'guardianship' is threatened, and invite others who embrace the same high principle to share in the responsibility to defend it, is a just act executed on behalf of all conscious Muslims, and in the universal interest of Islam's respect for mankind and all ideas that respect human society.[29]

The message was received by the rulers as a multi-faceted lesson characterized by high knowledge and understanding, humility, and uncommon wisdom.[30]

Today, it is a fact of history that the Royal Kingdom of Saudi Arabia remains intact as a nation-state and a regional power, and the War's outcome proved to extend Al-Saud family rule. However, the victory was not without substantial and bitter costs.[31] The intersection of those costs with the lessons employed by Saudi leadership to preserve their credibility in the Islamic world, converge today in efforts to create and sustain strategies that will effectively address the global specter of extremist Muslims and the threat of their influence.

The ideologies, symbolism, language, and actions of extremist Muslims from east to west threaten all civilized notions of society, particularly those shared by Islam and democracies. As during the Persian Gulf crisis, where Muslim-Americans articulated the principles in Islam which inform recognition of those shared ideals and instruct cooperation to defeat schemes which threaten them, a similarly critical, but overlooked, role exists for them today in confronting the various manifestations of this aggressive and dangerous enemy.

For the purpose of clarifying that role and creating opportunities for Muslims in America and other democracies[32] to serve their nations in the present circumstances, this book presents three primary areas for review and consideration: firstly, it recounts the socio-religious foundation and formative processes of the Muslim-American identity and community; secondly, it identifies and explains the Islamic principle of 'binding and engagement'[33] with supporting texts and references, for use as a composite tool to refute and nullify specific, misinterpreted concepts and terminologies associated with Islam that proto-extremist[34] and full blown extremist Muslims cite and embrace to justify their beliefs and behavior. Lastly, and most importantly, it aligns the aforementioned identity and principle so as to describe a potential and existing Muslim citizen-patriot, and moral agency,[35] prepared for a just service in defense of the truth of their faith and the innocent lives of citizens in their respective nations.

Part II: Identity

"And say: My Lord!
Cause me to disembark at a blessed landing place,
for You are the best of those who bring to land."

Holy Qur'an 23:29

3   Islamic Memory

"And say: My Lord! Cause me to disembark at a
blessed landing place, for You are the best of those
who bring to land."

Holy Qur'an 23:29

"He said: 'O my Lord! Help me, because they
deny me.'"

Holy Qur'an 23:39

As the religion of Islam and its growth in America[36] has become an issue of interest, study, and concern, it is now widely documented that significant numbers of Africans forcibly brought to America had been Muslims.[37] Though they struggled to retain some remnant of that cultural and religious life which slavery forced them to abandon, to refer to them as 'Muslims' in America is a misnomer. The nature of slavery in America was such that they could not have been any more conscious as 'Muslims,' as the term is understood in Islam,[38] than they were considered 'Americans,' as that identity was defined by the founders of the republic. The Islamic life they had enjoyed in Africa abruptly ended with their capture. Herded onto slave vessels as chattel and given no rationale for what was taking place, or possessing any awareness of where they were destined, the sense they had of themselves was shattered. Torn from their motherland, and in many cases advanced Islamic societies, they were marshaled as sub-humans into a foreign world; not as Africans nor as Muslims.

With the notable exception of a special few personalities, Islam as a viable expression of faith, community, or identity, was unpracticed, uncultivated, and unsustainable by slaves during the colonial, revolutionary, antebellum, and reconstruction periods in America. The Islam of Africa that many slaves knew was not transplanted in America.[39]

The noble democratic conceptions of justice, equality, and freedom of conscience, expression, and religion applied to all inhabitants of America, but slaves. The significance and impact of those rights on the slaves' identity was their awareness that whites did not estimate their value to measure high enough on the human scale to qualify for them.[40] Their nascent identity in America would be formed with that profound indentation; that as slaves and as blacks, citizenship status, albeit human recognition, was to be struggled for, and could be deliberately prevented, or held beyond their reach.[41] So, while it is true that "hypothetical Muslims inhabited the rhetoric of the Founding Fathers," the flesh-and-blood African Muslims-cum-slaves in America who lived in the founders' midst, remained invisible and without rights, hollowed by slavery, both as Muslims and as citizens.[42]

Persisting through slavery's destruction of their African, Muslim, and human identity, many slaves in America were able to miraculously hold onto memories of their Islamic past. Preserved in those memories was, not-so-much the details of Islamic practice, but, the imprint of experiences of Islamic life in high cultural and social achievement. For some individual slaves this was a vivid memory of a sophisticated Islamic social system, constructed and governed upon graduated Qur'anic precepts and religious understanding.[43] For most, however, the memory was more fundamental; recalled through the habits, perceptions, and attitudes acquired as an influence from the environment of their Islamic life in Africa.

Passed from first generation slave parents to their children as meaningful names, lessons of innocent faith, simple tastes, sage life-counsel, and instructive lore, that recollection of a past Islamic excellence would inform the development of lasting moral codes of thought and behavior, and eventually manifest in the formation of a new sense of themselves.[44] But, as long as America's "new birth of freedom"[45] remained complicated by a shrewdly constructed system of oppression that manipulated its victims to eschew any perception of themselves as free souls or intellects, or garner any respect for their humanity or citizenship among the general populace,[46] the development and expression of a healthy sense of human identity, whether Muslim or American, would remain a slow germinating process. Planted and nourished in America's conflicted soil, the seed of a new identity would stir with potential, but remain effectively dormant in public life until the early twentieth century.[47]

In the century following Emancipation, the experience of that cruel negation of the slave's natural human rights, which American democracy ostensibly contracted to protect for its citizens, and acknowledged for all human beings, would mingle with the distant memory of Islamic life in Africa, and cause a 'new birth' for Islam in the world.

Conceived in the society of liberty and justice that denied them such, the new Muslims would not be an imitation of their African ancestors, slave forbearers, or the Muslim world. The distinctiveness of their environment and pedigree would manifest through them independent perceptions, understandings, and emphases in Islamic faith, knowledge, and practice. Sprouting from the seed of the slave parents' memory, they would find Islamic orthodoxy, embrace it on their terms, interpret it within their own unique social experience, aspirations, and world view; and grow from the process into a new people with their own Islamic and American identity.[48]

4   Injustice, Hypocrisy, and Identity

*"Like a seed which sends forth its blade, then makes it strong;
it then becomes thick, and it stands on its own stem....*
Holy Qur'an 48:29

*"Do you see the seed that you plant in the ground? Is it that
you cause it to grow, or are We the Cause?"*
Holy Qur'an 56:63-64

As the struggle for racial equality in America grew from
the abolition of slavery and emancipation to striking
down segregation in the Civil Rights era, the Muslim-
American identity continued its development, breaking
fresh ground along the way. The contributions of Elijah
Muhammad and his harvest of followers to that process
cannot be overstated.[49]

By the 1960s, Elijah Muhammad had attracted tens
of thousands of "so-called Negroes" to his Nation
of Islam's 'do-for-self-and-kind' program of moral
upliftment, racial separatism, economic autonomy,
and religious and social identity reconstruction.[50]
Synthesizing the message of spiritual and material
salvation with race pride,[51] its bold, unapologetic call
to America's disenfranchised black community was to

join him, and embrace their 'original Muslim identity' with 'Allah's' assurance that the 'freedom, justice, and equality' historically denied them by whites in the 'wilderness of North America,' would finally be within their grasp.[52]

While the Nation of Islam rhetoric addressed white America's injustices towards blacks, its theology — W.D. Fard as 'God in the Person,' Elijah Muhammad as the 'Messenger of God,' the tampering of the Qur'an,[53] and anthology of the origins of race, the inherent goodness of blacks, and conversely, evil of whites[54] — simultaneously served as a summary rejection of the Muslim world[55] and its abandonment of American blacks who they knew to have been the enslaved and oppressed descendants of African-born Muslims. Underscoring the hypocrisy of the Muslim world within the context of Islam's burgeoning growth in America among blacks, was the irony that Saudi Arabia, the center of Islam, would only just abolish slavery in 1962.[56]

Both these factors — a rejection of the Muslim world's hypocrisy, and the African-American struggle for full citizenship recognition — would fertilize the growing Muslim-American identity. In less than a century from emancipation, an identity that sprouted from the fragmented memories of American slaves had begun a process of maturation that fiercely questioned America's willingness and ability to "live out the true meaning of its creed,"[57] and, exposed the Islamic world's weak commitment to the divine mission for which it had been originally designated.[58]

In 1964, three significant narratives in the Nation of Islam — all leading to the embrace of Islamic orthodoxy — would begin to unfold, further shaping the contours of the Muslim-American identity: first, the group's most recognized member, Malcolm X, was dismissed indefinitely by Elijah Muhammad from his post as minister of the New York City mosque, and National Representative of the organization. A few months later he disavowed Nation of Islam teachings as heresy, embraced orthodox Islam, only to be cut down by a hail of assassin's bullets in 1965. Second, American Olympic gold-medalist, boxer Cassius Clay, defeated Sonny Liston to become the heavyweight champion of the world and America's most well-known athlete. He subsequently announced that he was a disciple of Elijah Muhammad and a member of the Nation of Islam, rejecting his 'slave name'[59] in favor of the Muslim name, Muhammad Ali. He would later refuse a military service conscription order as a conscientious objector, be charged with draft evasion, and prevail in a landmark Supreme Court decision upholding the Constitution's support of his free choice of faith. A few years later he would also embrace orthodox Islam as a follower of Elijah Muhammad's son, Wallace. And lastly, that son of Elijah Muhammad, Wallace D. Muhammad, after completing a federal prison sentence in January 1963 for refusing, at his father's behest, to answer a Selective Service conscription order, was excommunicated from the Nation of Islam — the first of three times — for the heretical act of challenging the divinity of his father's teacher, W.D. Fard. He would later be reinstated by his father, and succeed him as leader, unknotting the Nation of Islam's teachings, reinterpreting its rhetoric and theology, and shepherding the largest mass conversion to orthodox Islam in American history.

The transitions for Malcolm X, Muhammad Ali, and Wallace Muhammad, from the Nation of Islam and its vitriolic condemnations of both an oppressive America and duplicitous Muslim world, to Islamic orthodoxy, not only influenced countless hundreds of thousands to do the same, but in a larger sense set the parameters for the Muslim-American identity. This conversion to 'true

Islam'[60] by blacks in America was not a superficial, nor superimposed, label for a 'black version' of Islam; nor did it come as a result, or endorsement, of the Muslim world's new-found interest in American blacks. It was a natural progression in the organic process of a maturing socio-religious, ethno-national identity, and an inspired exercise of conscientious faith.

Enabled by the external, historical forces of struggle for African-American equality and citizenship in America, and characterized by the influence of deep and reflective consideration of what Islam is, and what America promises, the embrace of Islamic orthodoxy by African-American Muslims stands as the most defining act, and measure of growth, in the development of Muslim-American identity. With it came the first stirrings of Muslim-American as compared with 'black' ethnic pride, values, and patriotism. But, more importantly, it ushered in the dawning of a new perception of Islam in practice, and would distinguish a new pattern of thinking for Muslims in the modern world: how to function properly and productively within a diverse social environment; how to partner with democratic ideals; and how to steward the promotion of universal justice and goodwill.

5   The Muslim-American

"It is a Qur'an which we have divided (into parts from time to time) in order that you might recite it to mankind at intervals: We have revealed it by stages."

Holy Qur'an 17:106

"If you want to know him (Muhammad the Prophet), he is the Qur'an living in the world."

reported by Aisha bint Abu Bakr,
wife of Prophet Muhammed

The acculturation[61] of African-Americans — the facts of history by which they have been defined, the attitudes developed thereby towards themselves and others, and the resulting contributions engendered to America — has carved indelible traits into theirs and the collective American psyche. One of those distinctive traits has been the influence of Islam, which as recited in previous pages of this discussion, has been palpable in the lives of African-Americans during the periods of their struggle for human and citizenship recognition. As Islam impacted their lives a niche for it within American culture has become apparent.[62]

America defines itself, in part, within the individual narratives of every ethnic group and their peculiar contributions to its national and cultural tapestry. The American acculturation process accommodates both the struggles of individual groups within the sphere of their inherent challenges and vis-à-vis other groups, as well as the record of triumphs and failures that ultimately distinguish those groups in the collective national conscience. It can be argued that blacks in America did not become Americans by the abolition of slavery, or the passing of civil rights legislation. While their citizenship status may well have been acknowledged in increasing degrees over time because of those hard-fought legal remedies, it was not until their group self-determination, of which those remedies were a part, became valued as a uniquely American story — that America could no longer define herself without including that story — that the measure of their American identity became equivalent to the descendants of their former slave masters and fellow citizens. Indeed, the acculturation process is not complete until an individual group's identity becomes an indispensable element in the national identity, and that group's sojourn becomes a metaphor for the nation's progress.

As Islam has evolved in African-American life, it has yet grown as an American faith. That is to say, Islam in America is neither racially or culturally homogenous, nor ideologically monolithic. It truly reflects America's diversity,[63] with its nuanced expressions that are simultaneously orthodox in belief and practice, and multi-pronged in understanding and application. To the casual observer the notion that Islamic orthodoxy can be interpreted, and acted upon, in various ways may seem a contradiction in terms; but the Islamic concepts of gradualism,[64] and 'observing the limits'[65] explain the many and varied expressions of Islamic orthodoxy in the context of Muslim-American identity and thought.

The concepts of gradualism and 'limits' establish that with an individual believer's recognition that every legal, social, political, or spiritual institution of Islam rests upon a divine ordinance that must be reverenced, he yet remains free to define himself as a Muslim within the polar limits of commitment to those institutions and obedience to the divine ordinance. The width and breadth of those limits accommodate and provide for a generous range of interests, emphases, and pursuits — all acknowledged and accepted under the aegis of orthodox Islam. So for the Muslim-American, the substantial space between the permissible (*halal*) and the forbidden (*haram*) is not necessarily restrictive, but rather, supports and encourages freedom of thought and expression;[66] whereas in extremist or proto-extremist ideology, that sacred space is occupied by pre-designated, coercive obstacles condemning any notion that a free mind has any part in the Islamic tradition. Muslim-American Islamic thought holds the greater of the space to be *halal*,[67] cherishing the prospects and implications for the exercise of a principled and disciplined free intellect that leads to productive society; while extremists believe the greater of the space to be *haram*, creating a maze of 'obligatory' impediments to confine such freedom, and demonizing it as the unrestricted and unregulated pathway to sin.

Drawing from the canon of Islam to further illustrate this fundamental point of divergence between Muslim-American thought and extremist ideology, it is reported in one of the verified hadith traditions[68] that an individual who had been taught a portion of the Qur'an by the Prophet himself was reciting it while leading prayers.[69] Upon completion of his prayers he was accosted by a senior companion of the Prophet. This senior companion, the illustrious Umar Ibn al-Khattab (who became the second successive ruler or 'caliph' after the Prophet's death), physically arrested the man, accusing him of the very serious offense of intentionally corrupting the recitation of the verses of the Qur'an. Umar Ibn al-Khattab took the man to the Prophet and leveled his complaint. The Prophet requested that the accused man recite the chapter of the Qur'an in question. After the man completed it the Prophet nodded his approval. The Prophet then asked Umar to recite the same chapter. Approving the accuracy of his recitation as well, the Prophet said, "This Qur'an has been revealed to be recited in seven different ways. So, recite from it whichever way is better for you."[70] To be clear, the true report of Islam shows even the most regulated ritual obligation — the five canonical prayers at stated times and the precise recollection of the word of God — to lend itself to a measure of freedom of expression. This reference further confirms Muslim-American thinking that elevates correct knowledge above rank,[71] intent above guilt,[72] sincerity above suspicion,[73] and natural rights above false piety.[74]

Muslim-American understanding of the proper functions and usages for knowledge in society is consistent with their interpretation of Islam's treatment and recognition of identity. Islam does not ask or require its adherents to dismiss their nativity: land, culture, or race.[75] For a Muslim in America to describe himself as Muslim-American is not to subjugate one identity to the other. Both are necessary and accepted components completing the Islamic and American identity. Islam acknowledges that the facts or circumstances of one's condition, or place of birth, are not of their choosing,[76] but are realities of existence, to which it ascribes teachings to be employed as potential strategies in addressing the challenges of a favorable or disfavorable environment.[77]

Islamic systems of understanding and practice grow from knowledge acquired as a direct result of individual and group experiences that pertain exclusively to environmental factors. As the great scholar of Islam and translator of the Qur'an into English, Abdullah Yusuf Ali explained, "It will be found that every verse revealed for a particular occasion has also a general meaning. The particular occasion and the particular people concerned have passed away, but the general meaning and its application remain for all time. What we are concerned about now [in the time in which we live]... is what guidance can we draw for ourselves from the message of Allah?"[78] In other words, Islam concerns itself primarily with guidance and the temporal choices of individuals and groups and their associated conduct, which ultimately qualify for successes and rewards, failures and punishments, in this life and the Hereafter.[79]

Muslim-American thinking does not advocate ignoring or casting aside the traditions, insights, and sciences derived from Islam's fundamentals by those learned devotees whose study forms the orthodox canon of Muslims. Likewise, to transfer the responsibility of navigating modern society's complex issues to the shoulders of scholars of antiquity is short-sighted and faithless. Muslim knowledge and identity is challenged in every age by that period's unique score of social, economic, political, scientific, and spiritual dilemmas. Western scholars observing the history of Muslim achievement and decline contend that the Islamic tradition of rational and objective observation and scientific problem-solving skills which ignited and sustained Europe's Renaissance have since been lost to Muslims in the modern age.[80] It has, no doubt, been the grandest struggle for Muslims over many decades to clear away antiquated bias from their lens of discovery and interactions with others, stand firmly upon the foundation in the Qur'an and Muhammed's tradition, but refine the focus of the lens to properly and proactively evaluate and act on the issues at hand forging alliances with civilized interests and building ethical coalitions along the way. The strength or weakness of Muslims in the modern world is confirmed by their ability, in the face of mounting problems, to adequately and skillfully apply Islamic remedies which honestly address those issues, and grow Islamic knowledge for themselves and for the benefit of human society. The perception that Islam is at war with everything in human society that does not embrace it, is wrong. At present, there is no more prodigious difficulty for Muslims, or the civilized world, than the fight for clear recognition of what Islam is and what it is committed to; and the fight against those who defile those sacred commitments, and threaten all others by their corruptive ignorance and destructive arrogance.[81]

The forming of Muslim-American identity—which for this discussion refers primarily to African-American Muslims in the tradition recounted—finds the Muslim world's commitment to fundamental Islamic principles of freedom, justice, and equality seriously deficient; and its ability to redefine itself and reestablish its moral commitments, without true Islamic assistance, improbable. This shameful condition, which is the clear reality of the descendants of Islam's first teachers, urges a rediscovery and renewal of the knowledge they misplaced, or lost. In his final sermon to his community, it is reported that Prophet Muhammed said, "All those who listen to me shall pass on my words to others and those to others again; and may the last ones understand my words better than those who have listened to me directly."[82] The 'last ones' to become acquainted with Islam, of all Muslims on the earth, are the Muslim-Americans.

This discussion has noted that the organic Muslim-American identity is the product of an enslaved people with an Islamic memory, mated to the society which once brazenly and exclusively denied them its founding promise to respect and recognize the inherent entitlements of all human beings. Within that crucible, a renewal of Islamic understanding was formed, and a new Islamic awareness bonded with democratic ideas has since emerged. Islam defines this process as *mujeddid*.[83] In this instance the *mujeddid* does not manifest as only one person reforming Islamic practice or pursuits, nor as a force of rebellion or revolution targeting adversarial structures or establishments. Instead, it takes the form of a people with a determined, sensible, and knowledgeable commitment to promote and defend democracy as Islamic.[84]

Furthering this discussion in Part III: The Principle is the presentation of the Islamic principle of binding and engagement; its explanation as a potential strategy to undermine the influence, dislodge the roots and growth, and disrupt the schemes of extremist Muslims and their ideologies in America and beyond. None have been better prepared than Muslim-Americans for the task of implementing it.[85]

Part III: The Principle

"And We wished to bestow a special help on those who were being oppressed in the land, to make them contributors, and qualify them to be heirs to establish for them a lasting place in the land."

Holy Qur'an 28:5-6

6   Security and Peace

"... and guard what is unseen that God would have
them guard...."

Holy Qur'an 4:34

It is universally agreed by all modern nations that among the most important pillars upholding society, if not the most essential, is security in its many forms. Not life, liberty, or prosperity can be maintained or sustained without it.

In Islam, and more precisely, in the language of the Arabic Qur'an — upon which the religion is formed — 'peace' and 'security' are bequeathed from the same source, God;[86] and are literally the foundation of the faith and the identity of the faithful. '*As-Salaam*', which is an attribute for God,[87] and the words 'Islam' and 'Muslim' are all derived from the Qur'anic-Arabic root *s-l-m*, which at once denotes submission, trust, security, and responsibility to foster peace. There are other Qur'anic terms which describe qualities and forms of security, but none approaches the universality of application as this term. Indeed, the regular and daily salutations of Muslims to one another as taught by Muhammed the Prophet — "*As-Salaamu Alaikum*" — translated, "Peace be upon you", is a constant reminder and affirmation to conscientious Muslims of their individual and communal obligation to promote the peace and security required to maintain civility and order in society.[88] So vital is this obligation that the Prophet legislated the salutation a formal right due from one to another, and the Qur'an instructs to answer it with the same commitment or better.[89] Reasoned from this perspective, verses from the Qur'an used by extremist or 'jihadist' Muslims, e.g., "If anyone desires a religion other than Islam, never will it be accepted of him,"[90] and similar verses — to justify egregious acts against any they deem to be in a non-Muslim category — can be challenged by more accurately interpreting the meaning to be that there can be no higher obligation in society than respect for peace and security (Islam).

Whether the Founders[91] of the American Republic can be described, or would have described themselves as religious, or Christian, or deist, or none of these; they understood that in framing the American disposition of mind and spirit, or character, they had to draw from the language of religion for its authority as a designator for the principles they found to best serve their idea for what the republic should be. Reverence to that Authority, however they perceived it, allowed them a natural and universally recognized platform from which to cite and justify such principles, and be heard and respected by other nations of the civilized world.[92] While the Founders' exposition of democratic ideas was singularly profound and original, they are unmistakably deliberate in assigning authorship of these principles to a Supreme Authority, who their language portrayed as Legislator, Judge, and Creator.[93] With the acknowledgement and welcome by other free peoples, the identity of a new people, the Americans, was enabled, providing an assurance that 'the blessings of liberty'[94] would be universally recognized and secured.

As this book continues, and introduces the Islamic principle 'wa rabitu wa jahidu' (binding and engagement) as a tool with which to address and defeat the influences and strategies of extremist Muslim ideologies, there is a fact that must be understood and appreciated about those who derived this principle and its perspective from the Qur'an and Muhammed the Prophet's teachings. Muslim-Americans came to recognize America's beauty and the potential for its form of democracy from a history of denial — denial of human and citizenship recognition and access to America's 'blessings of liberty'. The cultural and ideological resistance movement that was inspired by the thinking and rhetoric of Elijah Muhammad, that embraced his proto-Islamic Nation's message and rejected America's racist premises and its overt oppression of African-Americans, reached its maturity in 1975. Its group determination was reinterpreted by way of a new and inspired Islamic understanding. Likewise, its philosophy was transformed in light of that understanding and the finding of Qur'anic ideals of justice and community in the language of America's Founders. That grand adjustment and discovery was engineered, cultivated, and preached over nearly forty years by the primary architect of Muslim-American identity, Elijah Muhammad's son, W. Deen Mohammed. This point is not meant to be excessively critical or complimentary of America and her exercise of democratic principles. It is, however, to say that Muslim-American devotion to the security of the United States of America is a particularly pragmatic and informed allegiance to the American ideal. The principle of 'binding and engagement' is founded upon certain Islamic faith and knowledge, and a resolute embrace of the democratic ideas championed in America's constitutional guarantees. With a learned and skilled implementation of this principle Muslim-Americans make yet another contribution as citizens, and thereby cement a legacy that should secure 'the blessings of liberty for ourselves and our posterity'.

7   Extremism's Fiercest Enemy

> *"Fight those who do not believe in Allah, nor the Last Day, nor do they forbid what Allah and His Messenger have made forbidden, nor do they profess the religion of truth — though they are those who have been given the Book...."*
>
> Holy Qur'an 9:29

Muslim-Americans count themselves among the orthodox following of Muhammed the Prophet, citing the Qur'an, its true teachings, and Muhammed's tradition, as the foundation of their religious identity. This assertion, coupled with this book's explanation of the forming of Muslim-American identity, states unequivocally that Muslim-Americans are not a naïve, strategically-held satellite or cell in America ripe for the manipulation of foreign interests, leaders, ideas, or movements. Muslim-Americans are not fickle-minded pawns to be organized and activated according to the strategic designs, populist influences, or cultural prejudices borne of age-old grievances between the Muslim world and the West. Nor do they lack the discernment to recognize the difference between conflicts whose origins bear more the marks of national, regional, ethnic, or sectarian strife, than truly humane cries for justice and international Muslim assistance. Muslim-Americans are not the spiritual step-children of extremists who are programming and reaping service from the bodies and minds of an international army of ideological foot soldiers, and actively waging a selfish, terror-laced, illegitimate so-called 'jihad' against humanity and upon all democratic peoples and institutions. Muslim-Americans, by faith and conviction, stand against the delusional machinations of any present-day group's claim to a *shariah*-enforced, caliphate-led universal 'Islamic' state — firstly, on the premise that the Qur'an's natural 'Law of Settlements' or *'Qisaas,'* which grades the preservation of Life as a pursuit and duty above all justifications for taking life, plainly disqualifies them for any office of moral leadership; and secondly, upon the support and logic of the Qur'an-derived, Muslim-American developed Islamic principle of 'binding and engagement'.[95]

The above cited verse from the Qur'an is popularly interpreted by extremist Muslims to justify murderous attacks against innocent persons and populations they deem fit within the categories indicated, i.e., Christians and Jews in particular, but also persons not professing any religion, or Muslims who do not accept their ideas or authority. Any and all Americans "whenever they may be found"[96] would be included. These kinds of egregious misinterpretations of the Qur'an are a deadly influence wielded brazenly as authentic 'Islamic' teachings by the extremists. More detrimental and dangerous than any physical weapon, these ideas add impetus and recruiting power to the extremists' cause by suggesting divine justification for heinous intent and acts. Traditional Muslim scholars issue rulings condemning such acts, but their address is reactionary and not much more helpful than the general refrain of

Muslims that the actions of the extremists do not reflect 'true Islam'.

The only effective and lasting deterrent viable enough to unflinchingly address this influence is the singular power and authority of the Qur'an itself. Only it can expose and correct the erroneous interpretations, and destroy their influence in the minds and hearts of innocent Muslims or any other potential extremist recruit that may consider these interpretations to be true or accurate. In conjunction with a carefully implemented strategy derived from the Qur'an using the principle of binding and engagement, verses from it along with the authentic reports from Prophet Muhammed's tradition can be used to publicly and definitively refute all interpretations the extremists rely upon for their ideological foundation, and thereby weaken the gravity and magnetism of their ideas each time they are cited or become manifest. Websites and publications using this strategy can be circulated and their content further propagated through social media to confront the extremist ideology wherever it has presence or leverage. The key element of this strategy is that it employs direct references from the Qur'an and traditions of Muhammed without the muddling and interpolatory weight of commentaries. Knowing what verses to use and in what combination to address a specific ideological base of the extremists is a function of the principle of binding and engagement.

For example, in addressing the way in which the extremists interpret the verse that is the subject of this chapter's focus, Holy Qur'an 9:29, several more verses can be cited to either emphasize its proper meaning and context, or emphasize the incorrect way the extremists use the verse. The process need not make any mention of the extremists or their ideology. The verse(s) they use juxtaposed with the other Qur'anic references make the desired point readily. The validity of the refutation is made by the selection and progression of the verses. No references to one or another scholar or school of thought become necessary because emphasis is on the Qur'an itself. No Muslim will attempt to refute the Qur'an when the Qur'an is the only reference made. Additionally, the principle and strategy are effective in the original Arabic or any respected translations of the Qur'an in any language. In English, the presentation may read something like this:

I.   *"Fight those who do not believe in Allah, nor the Last Day, nor do they forbid what Allah and His Messenger have made forbidden, nor do they acknowledge the religion of truth — though they are those who have been given The Book...."*
(Holy Qur'an 9:29)

----

a)   *"O you who believe! If a wrongdoer comes to you with a report, look carefully into it, lest you harm a people in ignorance then be sorry for what you have done."* (Holy Qur'an 49:6)

b)   *"Surely, those who pervert the truth of our verses are not hidden from Us...."* (Holy Qur'an 41:40)

c)   *"This is a message sent down from the Lord of All the Worlds. And even if the Messenger were to invent any interpretations in Our Name, We would certainly seize him...."* (Holy Qur'an 69:43-45)

d)   *"That is most suitable: that they may give the evidence in its true understanding and interpretation...."* (Holy Qur'an 5:108)

e)   *"Then woe to those who write the Book with their own hands, and then say: "This is from God," (that they might) traffic with it...."* (Holy Qur'an 2:79)

f)   *"...those who distort the words from their proper places...with a twist of their tongues and a slander to faith."* (Holy Qur'an 4:46)

g)   *"It may be that Allah will grant love and friendship between you and those whom you perceive as adversaries."* (Holy Qur'an 60:7)

h)   *"And there are certainly among the People of the Book (Christians and Jews) those who believe in God, in the revelation to you and the revelation to them, bowing in adoration and respect to God. They will not sell the guidance of God for a miserable gain!"* (Holy Qur'an 3:199)

Admittedly, this is a limited example, as the Qur'an provides many angles by which to attack the extremists's purposeful misinterpretations. However, the publications that can be developed, transmitted, and distributed, most importantly, will tailor the selection and sequence of Qur'anic arguments against extremist ideologies simply by submitting their logic to the test and scrutiny of the Qur'an itself. This appeal will be directed toward the Muslim who is vulnerable to the extremists's twists and manipulations of Qur'anic logic and teachings. By filtering away their poisonous commentaries and leaving the unadulterated, straightforward Qur'anic message, that vulnerability can be replaced with conviction to dismiss, resist, and actively oppose the extremist logic. The identical process can be used with the authentic sayings of Muhammed the Prophet. For every lie or distortion that the extremists promote in Muhammed's name, there are any number of examples and combinations with the Qur'an that will refute and negate them.

The first of the pillars of the principle of binding and engagement — that for every corruption of truth there is an antidote, a healing, and truth restored[97] — informs the individual Muslim's sensitivities through which a proper understanding of Qur'anic themes can be applied. Muslim-Americans are true to their identity by proven devotion to causes of peace, justice, and goodness toward all people, which American citizenship presumes and Islam promotes.[98] These sensibilities, as an element of the Muslim-American character, explain the formation of this homegrown Islamic principle. In other words, it did not develop in its present form except as a result of Muslim-American strivings. Therefore, it can be described as the quintessential Muslim-American moral and leadership principle.

As this book continues to navigate the pillars of the principle of binding and engagement, it should be borne in mind that with new generations of Muslim-American children being nursed on this principle, and factoring their inevitable ethical contributions to America because of it, it becomes a gift of inheritance to all Americans. Sprouting from the genes of innocent Muslim-Africans imprisoned in the hulls of slave vessels destined for America, and now growing through their present-day Muslim-American descendants, this principle has been fired and consecrated by the spiritual and intellectual labors of countless great and unheralded souls. This book attempts to further magnify this principle for the benefit of Muslim-Americans and all citizens of goodwill.

8   Citizenship and Civic Virtue

"And We wished to bestow a special help on those who were oppressed in the land, to make them contributors, and qualify them to be heirs, to establish for them a lasting place in the land."

Holy Qur'an 28:5-6

The question of an individual Muslim's permissibility to live in a polity whose majority, or government, is not Islamic by its own definition and design; or permissibility to live under the authority of a non-Muslim ruler, or unrecognized school of Muslim thought or identity, has long been a matter of serious consideration, introspection, debate, and interpretation by Muslim jurists, thinkers, activists, and extremists, as well as non-Muslim commentators.[99] Whether a Muslim, strictly following Islamic codes of conduct, can be loyal to such described polities may seem absurd to Americans, or citizens of other Western nations, enjoying democratic conventions, where the choice and practice of faith is legally unobstructed, and matters of religious profession and identity are constitutionally safeguarded individual liberties preserved for all within the pact of citizenship. How an individual Muslim understands his faith, and his association with, and inclusion within, the international *ummah*[100] of Islam — and who, or what, is the primary influence guiding that understanding — can and will decidedly impact in what way he interprets his citizenship in a non-Muslim polity, and to what degree he is responsive, or responsible, to the interests of fellow citizens and the government where he resides. A fundamental argument of extremist Muslim ideologies, and most proto-extremists, is that no loyalties above or outside the "banner of Islam"[101] are morally acceptable or legitimate because, they reason, there is no prescription, standard, or interpretation of right or wrong, permissible or forbidden, to be respected, applied, or acknowledged by a Muslim, that supersedes the divine laws of God as derived from the Qur'an and traditions of Muhammed.[102]

This book claims no Islamic scholarly or legal authority. There are voluminous present-day examples of Islamic law interpretations in application in many spaces where Muslims reside on the earth, which, if a legal force were asserted for this discussion, would invite an analysis from representatives of those schools of jurisprudence, their legal rulings as adapted to those spaces, and the opinions of many Muslim strains of thought.[103] The point being that what Muslim scholars debate as legal or illegal does not necessarily dissuade or distract any Muslim, least of all, extremists, from their purposes, if those purposes have been formed upon convictions of faith. Nor do the scholar's deliberations necessarily reach or impact the process that an individual Muslim undergoes in defining his attitudes toward non-Muslims, non-Muslim governments, or Muslims who choose to live among non-Muslims and under the authority of non-Islamic governments. It is quite evident that despite the well-intentioned efforts of Islamic scholars, their religious rulings or *fatawa* have done relatively little to stem the rise and appeal of extremist Muslim ideas. In fact, in the scholars's reluctance to place extremists in the category of disbelief there appears tacit support for their objectives and attitudes. In evaluating the ideologies of extremist Muslims, the ordinary, individual Muslim will make a reasoned determination based on personal knowledge or access to what is readily available of what Islam advocates or disallows, to reject the extremist view as utterly un-Islamic, or embrace it to some degree. There is no middle ground in this choice, as many of the scholars admonish extremist tactics but acknowledge their beliefs as acceptable. It is precisely the beliefs of extremist Muslims that define their objectives and tactics. The individual Muslim that embraces any measure of their system or logic is locked into their influence and under their spell. What this discussion concerns itself with is not gaining entry into the discourse of scholars, but inserting Muslim-American thinking into the individual Muslim's thought process, and producing tools by which to reasonably guarantee that his choices will reflect a perception of Islam that places premium value on all innocent human life and civilized human society.

What is the basic principle defining Islam's disposition toward non-Muslims? This question singularly characterizes extremist Muslim ideologies. It is in addressing the implications of this question where the extremist's corrupted interpolations of circumstantial injunctions — found in the religion to define a defensive posture against polemical and physical aggressors against Islam or an Islamic community — provide rationale for them to designate all non-Muslims as enemies of God and Islam, and thereby treat them as immitigable targets. As a matter of ideological conviction, and in direct contravention of the extremists and proto-extremists, Muslim-Americans apply every reference from the religion that they cite to sweepingly categorize individuals and groups in the 'enemy of Islam' catch-all, to them, as a mirror of testimony exposing and condemning their non-Islamic attitudes, opinions, and conduct.[104] This conviction is taken from the second pillar of the principle of binding and engagement, and for Muslim-Americans, answers the question of Islam's underlying disposition toward non-Muslims. It is that all creation carries a natural predisposed urge to obey its Creator's design. Islam holds this to be an absolute and recurring constant that has repeated itself from the advent of the first human to the most recent birth of a baby to his parents.[105] For an individual to proclaim himself exempt of this natural law, or belonging to a category of nature other than this, is an issue of subjective, environmental influence, and not an expression of truth or reality.[106] Islam disavows the error, but respects the individual by offering "a wise and beautiful appeal."[107]

If Muhammed the Prophet had had the disposition toward those around him that the extremist and proto-extremists claim, then as Islam's first and foremost example, preacher, and ambassador, he would have won no support for his Message and Cause because he would have perceived them all as enemies without the capacity to respond favorably to him. If the picture the extremists paint of him was accurate, he would have had no logical reason for seeking friendship and recognition from a Christian ruler and society in neighboring Abyssinia (Ethiopia) to secure asylum for his persecuted following on the basis of common faith, effectively establishing Islam's first treaty of peaceful co-existence.[108] Prophet Muhammed's prediction that the Christian society of Abyssinia would treat his followers justly was not based solely on his knowledge of a 'Christian' justice system, but on his awareness and trust of the ruler's sensitivity for 'laws' of justice that prevail in nature. He recognized the ruler of Abyssinia to be one who respected the inherent entitlements due to all human beings based on recognition of their common human creation and common Creator. Thus, the Prophet understood, trusted, and promoted the principle that a natural law of entitlements signaling and requiring just, humane treatments must undergird all civilized and legitimate systems of law.

Indeed, this principle also figures prominently in Islam's specific recognition of the respect and consideration due to all peoples who have been oppressed, persecuted, displaced, and forced to flee from their homelands. The responsibility Muslims are obligated to shoulder in providing relief and asylum to such people is weighty. In this matter the Qur'an instructs:

> "And those who before them had stable homes and embraced the faith, displayed their affection to those seeking asylum, and do not hold desire in their chests for things given (to those seeking refuge), but gave them preference above themselves even though they were poor -and those who are saved from selfishness of their own souls- they are the ones who achieve ultimate success." (59:9)

In other similar verses and in an entire chapter (Surah 60 Mumtahanah - Those to be Examined), the rights of immigrants and the duties owed them by Muslims is addressed thoroughly and directly. Muslims cannot ignore that Muhammed the Prophet identified himself, members of his household, and his most senior associates, literally as 'muhajireen' or those who are fleeing or departing. In fact, the advent of Islamic life as a society of faith dates from the mass emigration of Prophet Muhammed and his following from Makkah to Yathrib -the settlement that later became Madinah and is known as the illumined City of the Prophet. The history of Madinah remains a stirring example of an established community selflessly addressing the needs of an emigrant population, and ultimately developing into a viable, highly productive, egalitarian society. Importantly however, the first migration authorized by the Prophet for his following was into the care and protection of Christian authorities in Abyssinia.

As Western and Muslim nations struggle today with immigration issues caused in many cases by the actions of extremist Muslims, reference to these facts citing Islam's teaching on immigration clearly distinguishes Muslim-American thought on the manner in which human beings who have been devalued and driven from their homes are to be respected. Muslim-Americans, as guided by Islamic principles, join with all civilized societies -especially those influenced by revealed knowledge- in studying the needs of immigrants, providing relief to them in light of what the best human traditions advise, what international resources will honestly support and sustain, and what the highest human conscience dictates to qualify as a just and humane treatment.

The third pillar of the principle of binding and engagement is that Islam does not desire interminable conflict with any group including those who are perceived as enemies. Islam acknowledges disagreement and contentiousness between human beings and communities, but does not sanction or condone any manner of ill-treatment. Islam accommodates conditional, but mutually constructive relationships with adversaries upon respect for the principle of free choices:

> "If your Lord had willed He could have made mankind a single people, but they are given to differences of opinion, except for those who God

has granted mercy. And for this they have been created." (Holy Qur'an 11:118-119)

Muslim-Americans do not view the world as a configuration of constraining lines defining the domain of Islam in confrontation with the domains of nonbelievers and disbelievers, as the extremists do. To the contrary, viewing the world in this way, the Qur'an instructs, is indicative of those whom are guilty of aggression and crimes against humanity.[109] The Qur'an presents the world as the domain by which God draws mankind together.[110]

The principle of binding and engagement acquires its name, logic, and approbation from composite references in the Qur'an, and related themes from Muhammed's tradition that encapsulate Islam's emphasis on constructing bonds of trust between Muslims and others. These bonds presage the formation and solidification of relationships which are intended to secure vital and common interests serving the support of the best conditions for human life in society. Additionally, these bonds, and their corresponding constructive techniques and strategies, do not contemplate areas of difference, potential conflict or dispute, above natural and obvious points of adhesion; and the verses from the Qur'an cited in support of the binding process qualify the purpose for the bond to be of greater significance than any aggravating issues, difficulties, or hardships that may seek to encumber the process.

For example, the fact that the United States is a majority Christian nation is not a justifiable reason for Muslim-Americans not to render their insights and other assistance to the nation during a time of war, as in the War on Terrorism and Violent Extremism, or other national crisis. In spite of the possibility of Christian distrust of Muslims for whatever reasons, or a climate of negativity surrounding Islam and Muslims, under the direction of the principle of binding and engagement Muslim-Americans are religiously and morally obligated to offer any and all assistance to the national effort until the crisis is abated. The principle acts as a philosophy of citizenship loyalty and civic virtue in times of peace and security; a defensive measure when society is attacked or threatened; and a weapon to defeat the commonly held enemies of human society. Even in instances of unavoidable conflict, the principle applies by insisting on humane, just, and honest policies of conduct toward enemies, with peace and justice as the overriding and superior objectives.[111]

The fourth pillar of the principle of binding and engagement insists that the only legitimate relationships to be constructed and maintained are those that are enabled for the good of mankind and civilized human society. By this reasoning, the 'rejecters of faith' or 'disbelievers' are those who conduct themselves in a manner that threatens innocent lives by effort and design. Even if an aggressor speaks words that align them with a specific religion or ideology, it is the evidence of intent and conduct that reveal faith, according to the teachings of Islam. The testimony of faith by Muslims called *shahadatain* or the 'two declarations', that is, to say "I witness that nothing is to be worshipped except God, and I witness that Muhammed is the Messenger of God," is more a declaration of action and commitment than testification of words. To be clear, saying the words and behaving in a manner contradictory to what the words are meant to convey nullify the declaration. It is more an action of the mind, heart, hands and legs, than of the mouth. Therefore, the behavior of a secular nation could be more in line with what is acceptable in Islam than a declared Muslim one. The philosophy of binding would promote and condone an alliance with a secular nation to condemn a Muslim nation which exceeded the limits of what is universally understood to be decent human conduct. Acting upon the axiom that a secular nation behaving justly is better than a Muslim nation behaving unjustly, Muslims observing the principle of binding and engagement would recognize the potential harm of such a Muslim nation, and strategically adhere themselves to the secular government in whatever function was needed, provided the activity did not violate general Islamic sensibilities. Islam, from the viewpoint of Muslim-Americans, does not make rejection of faith, or wrongdoing, the exclusive property of those who do not, or have not, declared themselves to be Muslims. Muslim-Americans would attest that the extremists and proto-extremists are guiltier of what Islam declares as disbelief, than those whom the extremists target as disbelievers.[112]

When the philosophy of binding is to be used as a weapon, it is an Islamically approved one that must be precisely and surgically directed at an aggressor and never involve tactics or desired outcomes that poison human environments, morally, economically, socially, or environmentally. For the integrity of the principle of binding and engagement as an agent of Islamic faith, it can never be deployed in the cause of a usurper or conqueror, only a defender of innocence, justice, and peace.

Specifically, the principle of binding and engagement identifies its foundation and borrows its name from four verses of the Qur'an. The following two provide its name:

> "O you who believe! Persevere in patience and constancy. Again, persevere patiently and steadfastly and strengthen yourself with bonds; and regard God, that (by this process) you will be successful." (Holy Qur'an 3:200)

> *"And for those who strive and engage for Us,*
> *We will guide them in Our ways. And surely*
> *God is certainly with the doers of good."* (Holy
> Qur'an 29:69)

As documented in Part II: Identity of this book, Muslim-American religious thought or methodology began in the crucible of struggle for human recognition and social establishment in America. It is the fruit of a morally determined people, and a product of autonomous thinkers. Some observers and critics have sought to discredit it claiming it is not properly endorsed by traditional Muslim scholars. But, to search it for the influence of traditional Islamic scholarly methodology as a way of disproving its legitimacy or determining the degree to which it complies with that corpus of knowledge would be the equivalent of attempting to argue the authenticity of jazz against a Renaissance-era Euro-centered musical standard. While it fits within the rules of the universal sciences which acknowledge and verify the legitimacy of strivings for human social identity, it has chiseled its own brilliance. Its language and sound stands to any empirical test. It is at once beautiful, unique, original, correct, and scholarly. It combines the highest classical understanding with the greatest spiritual depth.

With the bona fides of his pedigree and the loyal support of his following, it was W. Deen Mohammed who earnestly and urgently pored over Islamic sources of knowledge in order to grasp the disciplines that would define for his community a foundation to build upon, and principles with which to maintain and govern their Islamic life as an autonomous community within the international community of Islam, and in an American homeland.[113] By the processes of inspiration, observation, intellectual and spiritual curiosity and striving, study, and guidance, he acquired those truths and teachings. From 1975 to 2008 -thirty-three years- he fashioned them into an Islamic language environment and leadership culture that is responsible for the construction and philosophical support of the Muslim-American identity, and for the establishment of the Muslim-American model of Islamic life in society. What seemed to many -including some in his own following-irreconcilable conflicts between the perspectives of his father's teachings, the struggle for blacks for human respect and citizenship recognition in America's social history, and embracing an orthodox Islamic identity free from imitation of other ethnic Muslim peoples while promoting confidence in America and its idea of democracy, was instead for him a natural confluence of convictions of faith, universal moral and social principles, and the tribute to human dignity clearly preserved and advocated in the Qur'an and Muhammed the Prophet's teachings.

"THE IMAM," as we his people referred to him - and still do- taught that Islam and Islamic community are intended by God to accommodate and facilitate human progress in all human social environments. In some instances those environments may appear hostile or incongruent with Islamic beliefs and values. But, Islam applies and adheres nonetheless, and can function as a complementary ethical force strengthening an existing system, or as a leadership influence instructing human thinking and aligning human behavior with the dictates and requirements for sustaining a society of faith, justice, and peace.

In these contexts the Imam further refined and characterized the Muslim-American identity charting a brilliant and exact course from the limiting emphasis on racial identity that was associated with his father's teachings to an enlightened embrace of Islam's emphasis on human identity and potential. He contended that it was always his father's intent to introduce new understandings and foster improved possibilities for blacks in America, prodding and challenging them to become a healthier, more productive and established people. And like his father, he considered it a responsibility to invite all blacks to take charge of their own identity in America and free themselves of post-slavery labels that were wretchedly inadequate and superficial, and imposed by systems and philosophies unsupportive and insensitive to their best interests. He was among the first leaders to use and advocate the use of 'African-American' as a more appropriate term for identity, though he thought the term 'Bilalian' the most suitable and dignified. The term itself is drawn from the narrative of one of Islam's central and venerable personages -Muhammed the Prophet's trusted deputy, Bilal Ibn Rabah, whom he exclusively and officially designated to 'call' the people to their daily prayers. The formal Islamic call to prayer or 'adhan' is among the most recognized, celebrated, and lasting human religious traditions in the modern world. It is the symbolic action that introduces Islam to all of humanity and invites them to its perception of duty, worship, and prosperity. It is an ubiquitous human tradition, heard five times daily in every nation on earth, and is fundamental to Islamic faith and community life.

The narrative of Bilal's life proves rich for Muslim-American identity with its familiar historical and spiritual parallels. He was a son of Africa (specifically Abyssinia-Ethiopia) and a Makkan slave in pre-Islam Arab society, who heard and embraced Muhammed the Prophet's enshrined teachings on God's primary, absolute, and singular authority over creation. The Prophet's explanations of God's 'Oneness' enlightened and transformed Bilal, inspiring him to attend devotion to the 'One' God as his only true master. Thereafter, he openly proclaimed himself a Muslim, linking that designation with his inherent status as a free, human soul. He subsequently challenged his slave master's rights over him, vanquishing the psychological grip slavery had over his self-awareness, self-esteem, and self-interests.

The Imam's original use of 'Bilalian' as a term 'calling' blacks to a complete ethnic identity, alternative to 'Negro' or 'Black', welded a mythic bond between Bilal's life and role in the developmental period for Islam, and the tribulations and triumphs that have characterized the struggle of African-Americans. For him, African-American Muslims by way of Bilal's pre-eminence, have been justified and empowered by Islam to 'call' members of their own race, Americans of all ethnicities, and all human beings to the higher traditions of human dignity. Further, the term distinguished African-American Muslims as having valid leadership, membership, presence, and voice in the Islamic world. Some in the Muslim world bitterly opposed and indicted the creation and use of the term. But, its influence is one of many significant proofs showing Imam W. Deen Mohammed's leadership to have been an intrepid spiritual and social force guiding through the complex drama of fusing disparate elements of nationality, race, ethnicity, and religion into an identity. In no uncertain terms, he founded the legitimate Islamic identity in America, and secured a respected standing for it among Muslim peoples worldwide, as well as non-Muslims in the United States. The implications of this fact should not be underestimated as it pertains to the potency of the Muslim-American identity, the culture of patriotism and civic responsibility formed from it, and its relevance in combating the misanthropic ideologies of extremists.

Muslim-Americans who identify in this tradition live peacefully and productively by a treasure of social establishment principles alongside their fellow non-Muslim neighbors and friends. These principles are pervasive, rooted, and thriving among rank-and-file mosque-goers in the Muslim-American community, and promise to continue maturing into highly functional religious, educational, economic, and cultural institutions in America. Most noteworthy of these viable principles is that of 'binding and engagement', which explains Muslim-American social successes, the free-thinking spirit of the Muslim-American community, and the perpetual operation of an organic shield protecting Muslim-Americans from and against extremist influences.

There is no doubt and can be no debate that Muslim-Americans are orthodox in the most authentic Islamic sense. And yet, they cannot abide or do they approve or embrace the leadership of a Muslim world that fails every day in its obligation to serve humanity's best interests in the face of the modern world's demands and challenges to face down extremists.

The Islamic principle of 'binding and engagement' takes its spiritual foundation from the following two verses of the Qur'an:

> "... A sign of his authority is there shall come to you an object within which is an assurance of establishment from your Lord." (Holy Qur'an 2:248)

> "And We wished to bestow a special help on those who were being oppressed in the land, to make them contributors, and qualify them to be heirs to establish for them a lasting place in the land." (Holy Qur'an 28:5-6)

This book has referenced the unique acculturation process of American ethnic groups, who in belonging to other than the majority, became marginalized, targeted, alienated, isolated, and were otherwise abused socially, politically, and economically; but overcame those adversities, winning respect and acceptance, and contributing to America's strength and excellence. In these two Qur'anic verses from which the principle of binding and engagement draws its name, virtues of engagement, effort, struggle, perseverance, patience, and tenacity are all captured in the Qur'anic-Arabic terms *j-h-d* (struggle) and *s-b-r* (patience), which taken together suggest a determined moral commitment to some worthy objective. To succeed (*f-l-h*) in realizing that objective (i.e., "you will be successful;" "We will guide them in our Ways") the verses advise a strategy of interlocking or binding (*r-b-t*) with others who are similarly striving. Applying the logic of these verses together, and coupling that logic with an understanding of what feeds America's healthy national life, Muslim-Americans contribute to that life in the same productive spirit as other groups. Simply, they bond themselves to the process and to the objective as inextricably as any patriotic citizen, but with direct support from their source of religious guidance. The struggle to reach the objective of a 'more perfect union' and the concomitant acceptance by all groups to share in the burden of the inherent hardships further strengthen the bonds. Thus, success is the achievement of the immediate objective, but also the long-term cultivation of the bonds, which provide for a sturdy, enduring society recognizing many contributors and many paths of contribution.

Understanding this principle will close any philosophical gap that an American Muslim may debate concerning participation and cooperation in a sustained and energetic commitment to defeating extremist Muslim ideologies. This is an elementary component of the citizenship pact between citizens and their government. Islam places a very high premium on obligations and contracts of trust which all conscientious American Muslims must review as this nation engages extremist Muslims.[113]

9   Declaration

> *"Fight in the cause of God those who fight you, but do not aggress or go to extremes. For God does not approve or accept aggressors or extremists."*
>
> Holy Qur'an 2:190

In advance of suggesting of specific strategies for the engagement of extremist Muslim ideologies, and in order to remove any ambiguity regarding that which Muslim-Americans find objectionable within those ideologies and obligatory Islamic reasons to refute them, the following declaration of rebuke and intent to engage is made:

> "Muslim-Americans, in their faithful understanding and practice of the religion of Al-Islam — the proper name given it in the Holy Qur'an — do not recognize, accommodate, or accept the validity or legitimacy of any argument made in the name of Al-Islam or its sacred primary sources, The Holy Qur'an and tradition of Muhammed the Prophet, which seek to establish, foster, support, or give credence to anarchical or misanthropic doctrines in any variety.[114]

"Extremists, associating their ideologies with Al-Islam and its sacred texts in any manner, form, or manifestation, under any guise or label, for any personal group interest or cause, in justifying: [115]

a.) "The destruction of, or schemes to destroy, vital structures of human society, i.e., religious, political, economic, educational, legal, charitable, or cultural institutions, artifacts of cultural heritage, and physical infrastructures[116] within sovereign domains or other recognized boundaries; or

b.) "The systematic and illicit devaluation of human life or environments by active and open, intermittent, or clandestine and latent schemes of exploitation, abuse, or oppression, i.e., racism, sexism, classism, bigotry, impoverishment, unjust imprisonment or captivity, torture, forced servitude or slavery;[117] or

c.) "The willful taking of any innocent human life[118]; or

d.) "The willful taking of any life without justification and sanction of legitimate and just authority or cause,[119]

"is an egregious, absolute, and indefensible wrong; and an abominable, immoral, and criminal assault on the religion of Al-Islam, its faithful adherents, and upon all humanity which it is intended to serve."[120]

The proliferation and promotion of these extremist Muslim ideologies requires the firmest rebuke and refutation,[121] demands this declaration of intent to engage them with the best of which Al-Islam approves,[122] and obligates Muslims of knowledge and sound conscience to commit to this engagement until the influence of these ideologies are negated and nullified.[123]

10   Narrative of Joseph

"Surely in Joseph and his brothers are messages for those who inquire."

Holy Qur'an 12:7

This harsh and protracted season of extremism, characterized by murderous attacks on innocents and the anarchical rhetoric of so-called "Muslims" that invite and sanction them, has created acidic conditions whereupon many observers openly implicate the religion of Islam as the complicit, underlying culprit. Similarly, Muslims are accused, by association, as passively condoning these acts as part of what is said to be an ongoing, surreptitious plot of the religion to gain dominance in the world. While this may be a marginal viewpoint, for conscientious Muslims desiring to responsibly and intelligently respond to the horrors and the accusations, pointing a finger of blame toward the extremists is approaching, if not passed, the point of diminishing returns.

It seems that every Western nation is forced by the reality of looming threats and incessant acts of terror to fortify an already formidable culture of security that suspects their domestic and indigenous Muslim populations. Islam, in truth, seeks to guarantee society that its adherents be ever-vigilant in working for the good future and welfare of the general populace,[124] but the transgressions and crimes of extremist Muslims, and their ideologies which cite Islamic texts for support and motivation, display and argue the polar opposite. Under these conditions, even the convictions of the elected leader of the world's third largest democracy and most populous Muslim-majority nation, Joko Widodo of Indonesia, that "Islam and democracy are not incompatible,"[125] seem awkward and uncertain.

Unfortunately, the chasm dividing what Islam is to its well-meaning faithful, and what it is observed to be by security specialists in nation-states impacted by extremists' violence, and a growing number in the world's general public, is becoming wider and deeper with every passing news-day cycle. As implied in Chapter 9 of this book, for Muslims who care about the quality of their citizenship in Western nations it has become absolutely necessary to take direct, corrective action.

It is commendable, but predictable, that the response of many Muslim governments has been to more closely monitor their mosques and preachers for signs and evidence of extremist language and sympathies.[126] This strategy does little to alter a course that began with many of these countries's tacit philosophical, scholarly, and legal acknowledgement and approval of what extremists believe Islam to be. To the contrary, Muslim-Americans favor plans of strategic alliance and direct, ideological engagement.

For certain, Muslim-American leaders must keep their congregations and the general citizenry in touch with what Islam truly is by accurate preachings and campaigns for public dialogue and discourse. But, the seriousness of the climate obligates for a more surgical engagement. Extremist notions of the religion must be nullified, and Muslim-Americans have a moral responsibility to their country and its founding ideals, to their families and institutions, to their non-Muslim friends and neighbors, and to the legacy of those who lived and sacrificed for their recognition as human beings, as full citizens, and as Muslims, to see that the job is completed.

American Muslim citizen-civilians, and likewise Muslim citizens of other Western democratic nations, have no stated or explicit authority to act against extremist Muslims in the name of federal law, state law, or local ordinances except to protest their ideas and activities, and to report suspicions to proper authorities. It is not a productive strategy for Muslims or authorities to have the Islamic community become a den of espionage. In the long term this undermines the positive contributions a trusted and confident Muslim population can make to any democratic state, by creating an unnatural social environment. Trust and cooperation based on the common objectives sought by the state and the Islamic community that serves the immediate demand effectively is what is required.

Neither the state nor the Islamic community honestly trusts each other enough because of the climate created by the extremists. This condition plays into the extremists's overall plan, wherein they win more converts by pointing at governments and laws that do not respect their citizens and, therefore, will not truly accommodate or accept them as Muslims. This is a great burden on citizen-Muslims whose leaders are too often weak and ambiguous in their condemnation of extremist ideas, or who themselves emerge from traditions that are founded on the same premises as the extremists, and are, therefore, ideologically incapable of extricating or distinguishing their fundamental beliefs from them. It is for these reasons and because of clear, indisputable and incontrovertible evidence that a primary plank in the extremists's active plan is to influence and radicalize Muslims in the West to disavow and violate their citizenship trust, that Muslim-Americans are obliged to share more than their citizenship philosophy of binding; but also share considerations embedded in implicit Qur'anic teachings to directly engage extremist and proto-extremist ideologies.

Muslim-Americans surmise that most Muslims in America and the West are unable, for lack of knowledge, or unwilling, for fear, or lack of will and commitment, to see this mission through. The extremists know well that this kind of ignorance and complacency figures positively into the environment of confusion they feed upon creating more frustration and volatility between Muslims and the states they are citizens of.

Many who read this book will be well-acquainted with geopolitical struggles particularly as they relate to the Muslim world and the West. It is compelling that Muslim-Americans have been largely overlooked by fellow citizens and government officials as suited to winning the ideological campaign against extremists. Given their own well-known history of pushing away from marginal doctrines, embracing orthodoxy, and interpreting their orthodoxy to champion citizenship identity and responsibility, this unsettling fact poses questions that must be answered as our nation struggles with this enemy. If Native Americans, Jewish-Americans, Japanese-Americans, German-Americans and other ethnic-Americans were especially consulted and recruited to face down enemies with whom they shared some common facility, to gain tactical, if not moral, advantages in the campaigns of their day, then what prevents the same for Muslim-Americans? This book argues the great value of the Muslim-American community to the nation and its leadership at a serious moment in American and world history.

This book has discussed the Qur'an as a strategic Book. The Qur'an also speaks of itself as "a Protected Book".[127] This means that it possesses an internal 'trigger,' which when 'pulled' by some flagrant misuse will reveal an array of safeguards[128] to knowledgeable and sensitive persons for their use in preserving its textual and instructional integrity. These safeguards[129] can be interpreted to tactically expose and dismantle any scheme that attempts to 'shred'[130] the Qur'an's true meanings. This is not a reference to mystical or esoteric guesswork. Extremists's misinterpretations are a tangible influence on many innocent, but oblivious, Muslims to adopt incorrect modes of thinking and behavior.[131] In the hands of an experienced Muslim these safeguards act as a weapon of amazing clarity and effectiveness for defense against the Qur'an's misuse.

The extremist Muslim ideologies which mis-categorize Qur'anic injunctions and interpret Islamic law to justify immoral assaults on innocent persons, and to support the declaration of an unjust, un-Islamic war against democratic nations, their governments and structures, and their citizens of all faith communities, amount to a singularly sinister and vile use of the Qur'an. These transgressions render the extremists and their ideologies subject to the full force of the Qur'an's self-contained protective measures.

Muslim-Americans understand the Qur'an to be the inheritance for all mankind. Therefore, its protection is to also protect the proper understanding of the life it invites humanity to embrace. This act is a moral imperative undertaken by Muslims on behalf of all human beings.[132] To attack the Qur'an in ignorance, as many do in bitter rebuke of its misuse by extremists, is to be met by Muslims with knowledge and patience. But those who use the Qur'an in their diabolical schemes and ideologies of oppression arouse particular ire from Muslims who comprehend the enormity of the offense.

Muslim-Americans would never stand against any society which declares itself a nation "under God... with liberty and justice for all," because these are Qur'anic morals and values. Even if that society struggles to uphold and maintain those values, Muslim-Americans are duty-bound to assist and support them as an example to them of that which the Qur'an promotes. Likewise, Muslim-Americans are determined to oppose any who knowingly and purposely corrupt the noble aim of the Qur'an's teachings[133] or traditions of Muhammed the Prophet.[134] This is not an expression of over-protective love for democracy or Islam, or the Qur'an. It is founded upon firm knowledge that to work for the protection of the Qur'an's true message is to preserve the highest democratic ideals and to defend the notion of a free, productive society.

The most direct of the Qur'an's implicit protective devices are those contained in the twelfth *Surah* or chapter named Yusuf or Joseph. This chapter has many unique and special characteristics. It is the Qur'an's only continuous and self-contained narrative.[135] It also authorizes safeguards for the integrity of the Qur'anic message, the aims in the religion of Islam, and preservation of just human society, respectively. With a correct understanding, its applicable science conforms precisely to the need of any sincere inquirer.

For the purpose of this publication emphasis is placed on the language, phrasing, and themes in the narrative, which identify various schemes and ideologies that attempt to disrupt, subvert, undermine, or destroy the normal functions of a just society, as the Qur'an defines a just society.[136] The narrative isolates the characteristics and logic of each scheme or ideology, and introduces and applies the range and combination of remedies that defend and counter against them. It also conveys specific engagement techniques to address the schemes' variations, subtleties, and vulnerabilities.[137]

The Joseph narrative exposes the psychology and operation of several specific schemes of oppression in various manifestations[138] ranging from anarchy,[139] to devaluation of human life,[140] to ethnic cleansing,[141] to genocide.[142] It advises philosophical,[143] spiritual,[144] legal,[145] social,[146] and tactical measures to counter, defend against, and prevent such schemes and the ideologies which develop from them or seek to deploy them.

Because this country and other nations are faced with looming threats as this book is being prepared for publication, urgency demands that it identifies specific tactical measures highlighted by the Joseph narrative. These measures would include surveillance and intelligence gathering,[147] covert planning and deployments,[148] arguments for a temporary suspension of certain civil liberties in the interest of security and its related ethical implications,[149] general rules of counter-engagement,[150] techniques for de-radicalization,[151] and amnesty.[152]

Additionally, the Joseph narrative makes special reference to the technical use of Qur'anic-Arabic,[153] by which terms and concepts can be deciphered for their fullest meanings and applications. In what Arabic linguists generally describe as a consonantal root system, the original, basic idea or concept conveyed in a single, Arabic 'root' persists through many different variations and usages of that 'root'. With every word in the Qur'an derived from a 'root', in making slight changes to it the meanings are altered or refined while retaining a direct or indirect connection to the original meaning or idea. In this way, the Joseph narrative serves also as a key or legend to navigate and unlock other Qur'anic arguments supporting the same original strategies with an understanding or use more specifically attuned to the issues at hand.[154]

For example, a sovereignty may consider using covert tactics to address the threat of an extremist scheme, or an ideology, which may have displayed many variants. As with war, Islam does not promote or necessarily condone covert tactics. It grants conditional permissions to just and legitimate authorities on the credibility of their demonstrated use of the highest appointments of justice and moral duty, and only to guard vital structures for the interest of protecting a humane society. By researching and contrasting the many forms and usages of the Qur'anic-Arabic word s-r-r (translated 'conceal')[155] with its use in the Joseph narrative, the subtleties and nuances of the term manifest and, thus, animate the flexibility the term offers for effective use.[156] Using this function of the narrative improves perception of the schemes and their manifestations in multiple environments and circumstances, and enables more precise implementation of the remedies the Qur'an authorizes.

In its full context the narrative of Joseph contemplates many levels of assistance and essential insights for maintaining peace and security in society that is threatened by schemes or ideologies that seek to destroy it. In the specific context of this book's objectives, it provides much needed support for Muslim-Americans and their friends in effectively engaging extremist ideologies.[157] Due to its sensitive nature, we entrust and encourage a more comprehensive and focused reading of the narrative to the learned and the authorized.

Part IV: Focus

"You think they were united but their hearts are divided because they are a group that does not understand."

Holy Qur'an 59:14

11   Dismantling Extremist Doctrine

*"You think they were united but their hearts are divided
because they are a group that does not understand."*
Holy Qur'an 59:14

It has been our purpose in this book to answer three
primary questions:

> ➢ By what methods can the influence of extremist
> Muslim ideologies be nullified?

> ➢ What specific strategies can be employed to
> influence extremist Muslims to abandon their
> doctrines?

> ➢ Are there Muslims who have the knowledge
> and expertise to actively engage extremist
> Muslim ideologies in all zones of their
> aggressions against democracy; the sensitivity
> and preparation to carry and represent the
> banners of democracy and Islam; and the
> will and determination to prove successful
> through the plethora of challenges associated
> with the campaign?

This book has presented evidence and argued proofs answering these questions affirmatively, and with specific recommendations. In concluding this discussion, a final argument suggests adjustments to strategies in current operation, and further underscores the potential, but over-looked, service of Muslim-Americans.

Any strategies employed to counteract extremist Muslim ideologies—to address a nation's legitimate security requirements, or to calm the anguish of a victimized population's loss of innocent lives, or to broadcast the message that any and all plots, threats, or acts intended to subvert a just and peace-loving society will meet a firm, direct response—which do not inculcate lessons from a careful consideration of the recruitment processes and incubatory/preparatory phases of radicalization, will not satisfactorily abate their influence. In fact, by neglecting such considerations these counter-responses may unwittingly serve as a catalyst supporting the maturation and emergence of more virulent, resistant, and sophisticated strains of extremist doctrine. Of course, no proven subversive or destructive influence to the just and secure function of society can be ignored, and must be addressed in the interest of that society's security in the most effective and expeditious manner. However, leveling the capture or distraction of a handful of extremist Muslims—even leaders—against the hundreds or thousands newly recruited, and tens of thousands more profoundly determined and hardened because of short-sighted strategies, render the resources invested, lives of personnel and allies risked or lost, and the very justice pursued, to virtual meaninglessness.

To deal extremist Muslim ideologies a debilitating blow, the strategy must directly engage the primary philosophical weapon of their radicalization recruitment appeal and deadly motivation: the foundation of all extremist Muslim ideologies. Contrary to popular assumptions, that weapon is not how extremists practice and understand the language of jihad. As with all Qur'anic language, jihad is no less than a complex precept requiring more discussion than just these few lines. Though it has been culturally charged to suggest war, in its proper and careful reading it connotes moral struggle against a tendency that would weaken one's commitment to what is just, good, and humane. Ultimately, it can be understood also as a material, universal struggle against forces of oppression; oppression as defined in Islam being influences which seek to separate a soul from its inherent purpose and Maker. While the extremists wrongly interpret jihad to authorize sentiments for war, physical warfare, and the establishment of fixed war zones, it is the lesser known modern extremist interpretation of the *al-wala wal-bara* or patronage (of Muslims) and acquittal (from the evil of non-Muslims) doctrine that defines their absolutes for war – their rationale, their objectives, their means, their targets, and their enemies. 'Patronage and acquittal' sets the parameters and drives the techniques of radicalization. Specifically, it is 'patronage and acquittal' that prohibits and condemns the forming of bonds of friendship and solidarity with non-Muslims, thus, demonizing them, marginalizing their lives and existence, and making the extremist Muslim case for destruction of non-Muslim societies.

Depending on the group and its specific agenda, extremist Muslims will cite the doctrine of 'patronage and acquittal' to suspect, designate, and target all non-Muslims in separate, but intersecting categories. Those non-Muslim categories can target one individual or an entire religious group, philosophy, or political party. The categories can extend to include entire nations and their citizens, governments, or structures of society (political, educational, cultural, economic). Even

Muslims who identify with certain individuals, societies, or philosophies that have been placed in one of these categories would be an approved target by association. 'Patronage and acquittal' can be guised in iconoclastic, anti-colonialist, pan-Islamist, jihadist, anti-democracy, revolutionary, or any general anarchical language or activities. In all of its guises the extremists interpret it to identify any and all non-Muslims as an enemy toward which the rhetorical call for jihad is justified.

'Patronage and acquittal' pronouncements are drawn from specific Qur'anic verses which the extremists and proto-extremists interpret as the absolute and eternal boundaries between Muslims and non-Muslims:

> "Let not the Believers take the unbelievers for protectors or allies rather than Believers. If any do that, in nothing will there be help from God, except in this way you protect yourselves from them. But God cautions you about Himself — for the final goal is to God." (Holy Qur'an 3:28)

> "O you who believe! Take not into your intimacy those not among you, as of you. They will always work for your corruption and failure, and desire you to fail. Hatred has already come from their mouths and what is concealed in their hearts is even worse. We have made the signs clear if you will understand." (Holy Qur'an 3:118)

> "To those who take disbelievers for friends and patrons rather than Believers: is it honor that they seek among them? No, all honor is with God." (Holy Qur'an 4:139)

> "O you who believe! Do not take unbelievers as allies rather than Believers. Do you want to

offer God an open proof against you?" (Holy Qur'an 4:144)

"O you who believe! Do not take Jews and Christians for your allies and protectors, for they are allies and protectors for each other. And who befriends them becomes one of them. For God does not guide a people who do wrong." (Holy Qur'an 5:51)

"You see many of them allying with those who disbelieve. Evil indeed are their motivations and God has condemned them and they shall be in a condition of suffering. If they truly believed in God and the Prophet and in what has been revealed to him they would never have taken them for friends and protectors." (Holy Qur'an 5:80-81)

"O you who believe! Do not take My enemies and your enemies as friends offering them loyalty even though they reject the truth that has come to you, rejecting the messenger of God and yourselves because you are believers in God, your Lord. If you have gone out to struggle in My way and seek My favor, do you secretly love them? For I know all that you conceal and all that you reveal. And any of you that does this has gone astray of the dignified and correct path. If they were to get the better of you they would behave toward you as enemies, and act against you with their hands and their tongues with evil. And they desire that you reject the truth and evidence." (Holy Qur'an 60:1-2)

Hardened extremist, and the proto-extremist literature that created and promulgated the modern interpretation of *al-wala wal-bara*, 'patronage and acquittal,' will argue that these verses from the Qur'an have no constraints in their application, or context for their understanding. The extremists emphasize their interpretation of these verses as a central theme in their recruitment/ indoctrination techniques. They cite these verses in an attempt to argue the abrogation of other verses of the Qur'an and traditions of the Prophet, further calcifying their message of hate and destruction. 'Patronage and acquittal' is fixed as the primary philosophical doctrine for radicalization of Muslims by its reasoning, which says:

> ➤ trusting non-Muslims is absolutely forbidden because it denigrates God's favor on Muslims;

> ➤ any relationship with non-Muslims constitutes a categorical betrayal of Muslims and the universal Islamic community; and

> ➤ non-Muslims are deceitful by nature, loyal only to each other, and are devoted to undermining Islam and the Islamic community of faith.

The principle of 'binding and engagement' directly counters and challenges the notion and appeal of 'patronage and acquittal' on the basis of the Qur'an's direct assault on its faulty logic. 'Binding and engagement's fundamental Qur'anic premise that Islam does not require agreement on all matters between Muslims and Muslims, or Muslims and non-Muslims shatter the coercive tone of the extremist doctrine. Indeed, 'binding and engagement' promotes the truth that Islam is comfortable in a world of racial, cultural, and religious diversity, and wants to construct pillars of trust, fairness, justice, moral consciousness and responsibility, and civic alliances in society as the foundation for peace and security among peoples.[158] Principles which promote human cooperation across boundaries, and support every ethical way of accomplishing that task, simply put, are loved by God:

> *"God does not forbid you with regard to those who do not fight you for your faith nor drive you out of your homes, from dealing kindly and justly with them. For God loves those who are just.* (Holy Qur'an 60:8)

The Qur'anic verses the extremist Muslims cite to construct their abominable ideology cannot and will not radicalize any who are introduced to Islam, or become acquainted with it, by way of the influence of the principle of 'binding and engagement'. Further, those who have been influenced by extremist Muslim ideologies and, thus, radicalized can be engaged and brought to correct their understanding of Islam. As quoted at the beginning of this chapter, the Qur'an clarifies that though the extremists appear formidable and united, among them are those whose hearts can be penetrated with the truth, because "they are a group which does not understand."[159]

It is well established that Muhammed the Prophet was committed to building,[160] not destroying, human society. Muslim-Americans find this concept to be a 'lost property' in Islam and have devoted themselves, by example, to re-acquainting the Muslim world with it. It is in the best interest of America, Western democracies, and the Muslim world to acknowledge the immense value of 'binding and engagement' and Muslim-Americans. As the Qur'an says: "In the Law of Settlements, there is the PRESERVATION OF LIFE, O you People of Understanding."[161]

Muslims who consider this a defining characteristic of their Islamic identity and make it known to be such by their words and actions are certainly worthy of the trust of their non-Muslim fellow citizens if not that of their local, state, and federal governments. In fact, such individuals and congregations are among the finest communities to be found in any country. They carry with them an awareness and traits of citizenship responsibility -civic virtue and pride- that are seminal, and the foundation of an indispensable strategy that will aid our civilization in the great struggle of this age -the jihad against extremism.[162]

Notes

Author's Note to Readers: The following 'Notes' acknowledge and credit articles, speeches, and other original works or ideas referenced in this book. These 'Notes' are also a repository for my own personal extended commentary and thoughts. I have intended these 'Notes' as not only to cite references but to stimulate and enhance the reader's understanding of the book's subject matter.

Part I: Analysis

Introduction

[1]   Goldman, Adam. "Lawsuit: FBI uses no-fly list in bid to recruit Muslim informants." (The Washington Post, April 23, 2014).

> *"Awais Sajjad, a lawful permanent U.S. resident... learned he was on the no-fly list.... In exchange for working for them (FBI), the FBI could provide him with U.S. citizenship and compensation.... When he refused the FBI agents kept him on the list in order to pressure and coerce (him) to sacrifice his constitutionally-protected rights...."*

[2]   Ibn Taymiyyah, Ahmed ibn Abd al-Halim (d. 1283). "Majmu fatawa Shaykh al-Islam Ahmed ibn Taymiyyah" (translated

"Collection of Religious Rulings of the respected Islamic authority Ahmed Ibn Taymiyyah") (Rabat: Maktabat al-Ma'arif, 1980).

> "We know definitely that the Negus (King) could not implement the law of the Qur'an because his people would not have permitted him to. Despite that, he and all those similar to him found their way to the pleasure of God in eternity although they could not abide by the laws of Islam, and could only rule using that which could be implemented in the given circumstances."

Author's note: The above was written in reference to the Christian ruler of Abyssinia (Ethiopia), to whom Prophet Muhammed sent his followers for asylum, instructing them that the ruler there would not tolerate injustice and would be receptive and friendly to them. Ibn Taymiyyah is revered as perhaps the foremost scholar in antiquity to whom those of the Salafi sect rely for proper understanding of the religion and its practice. Here, his thinking reflects the notion that an individual or group can conscientiously live in society upon rules of justice other than those from the Qur'an or Islam; and earn God's pleasure while living among non-Muslims under non-Muslim rule. In other words, if a Muslim has believed that his purpose and struggle (jihad) in the world is to be demonstrated by a tactically open or covert resistance to, and destruction and replacement of, any belief or political system other than Islam; or that he cannot acknowledge or support the authority of any system other than an Islamic one; this reference affirms, upon Ibn Taymiyyah's authority, such a conviction can be legitimately opposed.

This opens an area of discussion from which principles may be derived that combat the ideas that: a) Muslims must interminably object to the influence and establishment of other faiths, political ideologies, or systems of governance; b) that they are prohibited from cooperating with non-Muslims in the pursuit of justice and; c) that they are prohibited from partnering with non-Muslims in creating, sustaining, or serving a just society.

1 The Two Sacred Mosques

[3]   A twenty-one member delegation led by Imam W. Deen Mohammed arrived in Jeddah, Saudi Arabia on January 13,

1991. The delegation was comprised of Imams representing congregations in most major US cities, as well as representatives of Muslim media, academia, and cultural concerns. The delegation was formally hosted by Prince Bandar Ibn Sultan, the Saudi ambassador to the U.S. Meetings were convened with individual members of the Permanent Council for Issuing Islamic Rulings — the high council of Islamic scholars, and its chairman, as well as the head of the Ministry for Endowments and Trusts and representatives of the Islamic University of Madinah. Meetings were also scheduled with Saudi and American military commanders and troops as well as an audience with King Fahd ibn Abdul-Aziz and Crown Prince Abdullah ibn Abdul-Aziz.

4   The official designation of the King of Saudi Arabia is "The Custodian of the Two Holy Mosques." This title confers upon the Saudi royal family authority over the maintenance and security of the sacred mosque at Makkah and the Prophet's mosque at Madinah. This authority is traced to the scriptural patriarch Abraham, who in Islamic tradition built the first house for the worship of God with his son Ismail: "And remember Abraham and Ismail raised the foundations of the House...." (Qur'an 2:127). This authority was later designated to the Quraysh tribe of Arabia to which Muhammed the Prophet belongs: "For the covenants by the Quraysh. Their covenants covering journeys by winter and summer. Let them adore the Lord of this House...." (Qur'an 106:1-3). Many Islamic traditions are associated with this responsibility, but the most significant of these is its tacit suggestion that those who hold this authority have special Islamic knowledge and are the leaders of the Islamic world.

5   The fifth of the five pillars of Islamic belief and practice is pilgrimage to the Sacred House at Makkah or *Hajj*. Considered an obligatory practice for those able to make the journey, an estimated twenty five million Muslims from all continents visit there annually for this and other religious observances.

6   Muhammed the Prophet was born in Makkah. After receiving his divine mission he migrated with a group of his followers to Madinah to escape persecution. Over twenty three years of his adult life, Islamic tradition holds that God revealed the Qur'an to him by way of the angel Gabriel. In Madinah he established the prototypal model of Islamic society. Thus, the basis of Islamic faith and practice are the teachings of the Qur'an

and Prophet Muhammed's sayings, decisions and actions as leader of the Islamic community. This record is sanctified and amplified in the cities formally known as Makkah, the Blessed and Madinah, the Illumined.

[7]   The political ideology of Saddam Hussein's Iraq was Ba'athism. Derived from an Arabic word meaning "resurrection" its adherents were also the ruling party in Hafez al-Assad's Syria and remain in power today under his son Bashar. Ba'athism (or the Ba'ath Party), as conceived by Michel Aflaq, a Christian Arab, combines the rhetoric of Arab nationalism, pan-Arabism, and Arab socialism, and calls for the unification of the Arab world into a single state. It is considered heretical by Islamic authorities due to its flirtations with Marxist ideas that condemn religious faith, and its zealous preoccupation with Arab unity.

[8]   Authority over the Holy Precincts of Makkah and Madinah has long been an issue debated and disputed by Islamic authorities. It is generally argued that the sacred areas of Islam are the responsibility of the international Muslim faithful and should be maintained in trust by a body representative of the Muslim world, and selected by a consensus of Islamic authorities. With the creation of the modern Saudi state and its international recognition after World War One, the Holy Precincts' designation as a protectorate under Ottoman and other Arab authorities was nullified in favor of the ruling Al-Saud monarchy. Many Muslims then (including some of those once loyal to the first king of Saudi Arabia, Abd al-Aziz Ibn Saud) and now, considered aspects of that recognition, particularly the Al-Saud relationship with Great Britain, as inappropriate interference in matters of Islamic faith by non-Muslims, thereby, regarding the authority of the Al-Saud family over the Holy Precincts as illegitimate.

[9]   "The Holy Qur'an"

> "O you that believe! Betray not the trust of Allah and the Messenger, nor misappropriate knowingly things entrusted to you." (8:27)

> "How can there be a league before Allah and His Messenger, with the pagans, except those with whom you made a treaty near the Sacred Mosque? As long as these stand true to you, stand you true to them...." (9:7)

> *"Fulfill the Covenant of Allah when you have entered into
> it, and break not your oaths after you have confirmed them:
> Indeed, you have made Allah your surety...."* (16:91)

Author's note: Agreements, oaths, trusts, treaties, and the like,
when agreed upon in good faith are binding and enforceable
between Muslims themselves, and non-Muslims, alike. One of the
names attributed to Muhammed the Prophet by his followers, and
adversaries, was Al-Amin, which translates 'the one who keeps
his trusts.'

[10] Ibid.,

> *"Fight in the cause of Allah those who fight you,
> but do not transgress limits; for Allah does not love
> transgressors."* (2:190)

> *"But when He delivers them, Behold! they transgress
> insolently through the earth in defiance of what is
> right! O mankind! your insolence is against your own
> souls...."* (10:23)

> *"The blame is only against those who oppress men with
> wrongdoing and insolently transgress beyond bounds
> through the land, defying right and justice; for such there
> will be a grievous penalty."* (42:42)

[11] Ibid.,

> *"But what plea have they that Allah should not punish them,
> when they keep men from the Sacred Mosque, and they are
> not its guardians? No men can be its guardians except the
> righteous; but most of them do not understand."* (8:34)

[12] Ibid.,

> *"As to those who have rejected Allah, and would keep back
> men from the Way of Allah, and from the Sacred Mosque,
> which We have made open to all men - equal is the dweller
> there and the visitor from the country, and any whose
> purpose therein is profanity or wrongdoing, them We will
> cause to taste a most grievous penalty."* (22:25)

[13]   Sahih al-Bukhari.

> 914. *"...There will be no town in which the Great Deceiver will not enter except Makkah and Madinah...."*

[14]   Worth, Robert. "The Deep Intellectual Roots of Islamic Terror." (The New York Times, October 13, 2001)

> *"(Osama bin Laden argues that the) Saudi government, which earned his wrath by expelling him and serving as host to American troops during the Persian Gulf War, is illegitimate. 'By opening the Arab peninsula to the crusaders, the regime disobeyed and acted against what has been enjoined by the messenger of God,' Mr. bin Laden wrote in his 1996 'Declaration of War Against America.' In so doing, the Saudi leaders ceased to be Muslims, he concluded. That message resonates even with Muslims who do not share Mr. bin Laden's extreme views, largely because many Arabs see not just the Saudi regime but the entire political order in the Arab world today as tyrannical and corrupt...."*

[15]   King Abd al-Aziz Ibn al-Saud, recognized internationally as absolute monarch in 1927 by the Treaty of Jeddah, was opposed to further expansion into regional territories not already in his dominion (especially those protected by the British). Leading members of his own elite forces (the Ikhwan) regarded this decision as capitulation to British interests. The schism developed into a full-scale insurgency that threatened Al-Saud authority. The rebellion was ultimately put down in 1929 at the Battle of Sabilla.

2 An Overlooked Role

[16]   The senior Islamic scholars of the Kingdom of Saudi Arabia belong to a committee called 'The Permanent Council for Islamic Research and Issuing Religious Rulings.' It serves as an advisory body to the rulers, and others who are responsible for governmental ministries, i.e., defense, education, etc. The 'Permanent Council' is also considered by many learned Muslims to be the highest Islamic legal authority in the world, and to which Muslim scholars, leaders, and common

people from other nations refer for *fatawa* (*fatwa*, singular) or religious rulings.

17   The leader of the delegation was W. Deen Mohammed, son of Elijah Muhammad, who had succeeded his father as leader of the 'Nation of Islam' in 1975 (another organization also termed 'Nation of Islam' was founded by Louis Farrakhan after he broke from W. Deen Mohammed's following in 1978). He is credited with correcting the erroneous religious ideas of the 'Nation' to conform with orthodox Islamic tradition, and transforming Elijah Muhammad's organization and following into the largest Islamic community in the western hemisphere. He is the primary influence in the formation of Muslim-American identity as it is defined and referenced in this book. The breadth of his influence as both an American religious leader and international Islamic leader is difficult to measure as the changes he fostered among American Muslims have had an impact on Muslims of every continent. In many quarters, including Saudi Arabia, he was spoken of as a modern-day *mujeddid** or reformer, and a leading figure in the serious discussion for the development of a distinctly American school of Islamic religious thought or *madhhab*.

The late, respected Christian scholar, Dr. C. Eric Lincoln, author of the seminal work "Black Muslims in America," wrote of him:

> *"The world stood in astonishment when Wallace Deen Mohammed renounced the political leadership of the Nation of Islam with its plush securities and emoluments and chose rather the spiritual leadership of the Muslim Community in the West. His was not merely a gesture of symbolism, but a clear and clarion public commitment to a religious investment reaching far beyond the accidents of the world today and tomorrow, and anchoring the well-being of his followers in the solid rock of classical Islam."*

*Author's note: More information on this term as it relates to the information of Muslim-American identity is discussed in Part II of this book.

18   The term 'Muslim-American' in general refers to Muslims in America and is used interchangeably with other terms, i.e., 'American Muslims.' In public discourse its usage tends

to describe both immigrant and indigenous populations who are citizens of the United States and identify Islam as their faith. The complexities of Islam in America can be blurred by the interchangeable use of these terms and their respective meanings. The term 'American Muslim' indicates an identification with the beliefs and practices of mainstream Islam within the plural religious environment of America, while 'Muslim-American' signals an ethnic identity and a rejection of sectarian labels like Sunni, Shia, or Salafi, in favor of an interpretation of orthodox Islamic life and practice tailored especially for Muslims in American society.

For the specific purposes of this book my use of the term refers to the latter, as that identity has evolved among African-Americans who associate themselves with the orthodox teachings of Islam under the leadership of W. Deen Mohammed; and other ethnic groups of Muslims who identify their Islamic life as inextricably intertwined with their American nationality and citizenship.

To be clear, the first publicly recorded use of the term 'Muslim-American' was by W. Deen Mohammed to officially describe the community he represented on the occasion of the "First Liberty Summit" hosted by the Williamsburg Charter Foundation in 1988. The summit ceremony commemorated the significance of the First Amendment guarantee of freedom of religion. Joined by the Christian evangelist Billy Graham and representatives of other faiths, Imam Mohammed signed a 'reaffirmation' of support of the 'first liberty'. On that document he identified himself as "Son of Elijah (Poole) Muhammad and Clara (Evans) Muhammad, Leader in the Society of Muslim-Americans," and gave the following statement.

> *"Precious souls of Americans from the past and you who are gathered here, I greet you as Muslims greet each other, 'Peace be unto you.' The following is given as an expression of Muslims' deep-seated support for the freedom of religion:*
>
> *"The Founding Father's classic treatment of man's worth and American law in its constitutional role of championing the safety of man's common and vital life and liberty, are no doubt concerns held in sacred regard by the international*

community of Muslims. Moreover, that our holy book, the Koran, and our Prophet, peace be upon him, Muhammed, represents for Muslims the living and enduring sources of our support for freedom of religion, is common knowledge with Muslims of all nationalities.

"Therefore, it is in the spirit of man's historical, classic, and universal attention to human life and freedom of religion that we humbly join the Williamsburg Charter Foundation reaffirmation ceremony. With the many races and religions of America, we cherish for all others, as we do for ourselves, the first liberty."

[19]   Imam W. Deen Mohammed and the Muslim-American delegation met individually with members of the 'Permanent Council for Islamic Research and Issuing Religious Rulings,' as well as select government officials and members of the Saudi Royal family. In addition to the King (Fahd Bin Abd al-Aziz), the Crown Prince (Abdullah Ibn Abd al-Aziz), and the defense minister (Prince Sultan Ibn Abd al-Aziz), noted among those that requested meetings with the delegation were the chief member and chairman of the council: the renowned Abd al-Aziz Ibn Baz, Grand Mufti of the Kingdom, and bastion of Islamic knowledge in the Wahhabi-Salafi-Sunni tradition. Other members that met with the delegation were scholars Muhammad Ibn al-Uthaymeen and Saalih al-Fawzaan. Government officials that hosted meetings were Muhammad ibn Hadee al-Makhalee, Chancellor of the Muhammad Ibn Saud University and Abdullah Ibn al-Turki, Minister for the Department of Endowments and Trusts. Imam Mohammed also addressed the international conference of Islamic scholars and leaders.

[20]   Author's note: According to the Qur'an, Islam's notion of a just society builds first from God's respect for the will and choice of the human being to recognize and accept Him without His authority being imposed:

"O you who believe! Upon you is the responsibility for yourselves." (5:105)

> *"And had your Lord willed, all those on earth would have believed together. So will you then compel mankind until they become believers?"* (10:99)

> *"There is no compulsion in religion. Surely, the correct path is distinct from the wrong one."* (2:256)

> *"Say: Believe in it or do not believe in it...."* (17:107)

Secondly, the individual's life in society is maintained and protected by mores of reasoning and behavior which are based on principles of fairness and equity and can be codified into laws by legitimate governing authorities:

> *"Thus, We have made you a society justly balanced...."* (2:143)

> *"O you who believe, stand out firmly for justice as witnesses to God, even when against yourselves, or your parents, or your kin, and whether it be in favor of rich or poor: for God can best protect both. Follow not the desire (in your hearts) lest you swerve and distort or decline to do justice...."* (4:135)

> *"O you who believe! Stand out firmly for God as witnesses to fairness, and let not the hatred of others toward you make you swerve to wrong and depart from justice. Be just; that is next to piety...."* (5:8)

> *"Let there arise from you a society of people inviting to all that is good, encouraging what is right and forbidding what is wrong...."* (3:104)

Lastly, authorities or rulers are not divine and do not rule by divine right. They share, along with the general members of society, in the observance and administration of these codes of morality as trustees, and rule with the consent and support of the people, and consciousness of God's Authority over all of them:

> *"Do you have an absolute authority? Then bring your Book if you are truthful!"* (37:156-157)

> *"O you who believe! Obey God and obey the Messenger, and those charged with authority among you. If you differ*

among yourselves refer it to God and His Messenger, if you do believe in God and the Last Day. That is best and most suitable for final determination." (4:59)

21 Author's Note: According to the Qur'an, just governments owe a loyal citizenry:

a) To provide an environment that promotes peace, unity, and prosperity:

> *"To each is a goal to which God turns him; then strive together as in a race towards all that is good...."* (2:148)

> *"O you who believe, persevere consistently and patiently. Work together in that perseverance and strengthen each other; be regardful of God (in all of that) and you will prosper."* (3:200)

b) Obedience to the citizenship pact made between them and their people:

> *"God commands you to render back your trusts to whom they are due...."* (4:58)

> *"O you who believe, betray not the trust of God and His Messenger; nor knowingly misappropriate that which is entrusted to you."* (8:27)

c) To be vigilant and prepared to defend and protect citizens against tyranny and all enemies:

> *"Against (those that threaten) make ready your strength to the utmost of your power...."* (8:60)

> *"But indeed if any do help and defend themselves after a wrong is done to them, against such there is no cause of blame. The blame is only against those who oppress men with wrongdoing and transgress beyond bounds through the land defying right and justice."* (42:41-42)

> *"And fight them until there is no more tribulation and oppression, and there prevail justice and faith in God; but if*

> *(trouble) ceases let there be no hostility, except to those who are oppressors."* (2:193)

[22]   Locke, John. "A Letter Concerning Toleration." (Excerpt, circa 1650).

> *"Nay, if we may openly speak the Truth and as becomes one Man to another, neither Pagan, nor Muhametan (Muslim), nor Jew ought to be excluded from the Civil Rights of the Commonwealth...."*

> *"No private person has any Right in any manner, to prejudice another Person in his Civil Enjoyments... All Rights and Franchises belong to him as a man... inviolably preserved to him."*

Author's Note: Perhaps the most important influence on Thomas Jefferson and others of the Founding Fathers of the United States was the English social philosopher John Locke and his writings on natural human rights and freedoms, and how governments should treat them. Writing in defense of freedom of religion and conscience in his "An Essay Concerning Toleration," he contended that the individual's relationship to God posed no danger to society, and in fact contributed to it; and the state should therefore have no control over religion. A few years later in his widely known "A Letter Concerning Toleration," he wrote the words quoted above concluding that no individual should be "excluded" from respect in society and that recognition for his individual choices are an inviolable right. These words respecting the human individual in society would be echoed nearly a century later in the ideas Thomas Jefferson conveyed in the "Statute of Virginia for Religious Freedom," where he wrote:

> *"... That therefore the proscribing any citizen as unworthy the public confidence... unless he profess or renounce this or that... opinion, is depriving him injuriously of those privileges and advantages to which, in common of his fellow citizens, he has a natural right."*

These and the lasting proclamations made by the Declaration of Independence as to mankind's endowment of "certain unalienable Rights...." are recognized to be the cornerstone ideas of American democracy and shared alike with all democratic societies and governments.

23   Author's note: According to the Qur'an, the human individual is acknowledged by his Creator as a creature with inherent excellence, dignity, and purpose:

> *"We have created mankind in the most excellent mould."* (95:4)

> *"...No laborer can take from another's labor. That man can have nothing but what he labors for, and the fruits of his labor will come into focus. Then he will be rewarded with a complete reward."* (53:38-41)

> *"By the soul (human self), and its perfect shape and balance, and its enlightenment as to what is wrong and right for it. Truly he succeeds who cares for it, and he fails who neglects it."* (91:7-10)

24   Author's note: According to the Qur'an, mankind holds the elite station in the creation of God:

> *"It is We who have placed you with authority on earth and provided you with the means for the fulfillment of your life."* (7:10)

> *"It is He who created for you all things on earth...."* (2:29)

25   Author's note: According to the Qur'an, mankind is entrusted with special responsibility and given special favor:

> *"We have made honorable the children of Adam... and conferred upon them special rights...."* (17:70)

26   Author's note: According to the Qur'an, there are others besides Muslims, who recognize, value, and are prepared to protect the life and liberty that God intended for human beings to enjoy:

> *"And there are certainly among the People of the Book those who believe in God, in the revelation to you, and in the*

> *revelation to them, bowing in humility to God: they will not sell the signs of God for a miserable gain...."* (3:199)

[27] Author's note: Those societies which extol principles that elevate and respect the human individual and safeguard human life are heralded in the Qur'an:

> *"As to the righteous they will be in the sanctuary of security."* (44:51)

> *"And for such as honor the time when they will stand before the sanctuary of their Lord, there will be two gardens."* (55:46)

[28] The Holy Quran

> *"Remember We made the House a place of assembly for men and a place of safety...."* (2:125)

> *"... Have We not established for them a secure sanctuary...?"* (28:57)

> *"The first House appointed for mankind was that at Bakkah, full of blessings and of guidance for all. In it are manifest signs... whoever enters it attains security...."* (3:97)

> *"From wherever you originate turn your face in the direction of the Sacred Mosque; and wherever you are turn your face toward it that there be no ground of dispute against you among the people, except those that are bent on wrongdoing. Fear them not, but regard Me; that I may complete my favor on you, and you may be guided."* (2:150)

[29] Fundamentally, Islam promotes respect for all people. The Qur'an says:

> *"God created the heavens and the earth for just ends, and in order that each soul may find the compensation of what it has earned and none of them will be disrespected."* (45:22)

30 W. Deen Mohammed delivered the following statement on January 18, 1991 at the International Islamic Conference on the Persian Gulf Crisis in Makkah, Saudi Arabia:

> "With the Name Allah, the Merciful Benefactor, the Merciful Redeemer. Praise belongs to Allah, the Cherisher and Sustainer of the worlds. We ask Allah for assistance and we beg His forgiveness. We believe in Him, the Sublime, the Glorious. We worship none but Him, even though the disbelievers are averse.

> "The Prayers and the Peace be upon Muhammed Ibn Abdullah, the generous Messenger. The Prayers and the Peace be upon him, and his Companions all, and what follows.

> "O esteemed Brothers! The Peace and Blessings of Allah be upon you.

> "The invitation from Rabita (Muslim World League) honors us as does King Fahd bin Abdul-Aziz and the kingdom of Saudi Arabia.

> "In addressing the cruel burden put upon the Kuwaiti rulers, their citizens, their guests, their families, their women and children, this statement asks that Iraqi aggressors and Arab governments remember more of Islam and Islamic history and sin less.

> "I won't be giving my attention to your faces. Normally I don't look at faces of people of an audience that I consider to be above me in knowledge of the matter at hand. So, I won't be looking at your faces.

> "Remember, our brothers, the hands of the man in the story recorded by Bukhari. He was walking with his hands to the skies to say, 'Religious people look at my misery. This religion is not fair.' To this man's tricky complaints, our Prophet, the prayers and the peace be upon him, said, 'How can help come to you from Allah while your food is haram (forbidden) and your dress is haram?'

"I don't want to disturb your sense of dignity. Remember whatever your Arab ancestors achieved of power and glory before Al-Islam was not something that could rescue you during the days of Jahiliyah (the days of ignorance and darkness and oppression of Arab souls and intellects). A remnant for your rescue was among you in Muhammed, called 'El-Amin.' Allah, the Qur'an, Muhammed the last Prophet, the religion of Al-Islam rescued you.

"Arabs, our esteemed models in Islamic history, before you were saved and raised up to glory by your religion, by Islam which is also my religion, you had your lands and you had your governments. Remember what occurred to transform your life and caused the eyes of other nations to look up to you was not your past glory but it was your transformed lives. It was your religion, your Islam.

"Arab leaders, our leaders, my brothers. I am a student of history and religion. I have come to know the ancient Arabian historical greatness to value and applaud your place in history. I have a strong admiration for the Arab people in the history of civilization. However, I have what I think is a sober admiration for you.

"At this conference we have been informed. Though the burden of our Palestinian brothers is no less painful for us, our position in regards to the occupation of Kuwait is that the forces of Iraqi (Saddam Hussein) occupation should withdraw unconditionally. Their presence there is not acceptable.

"Remember, clever enemies do more than just study our weaknesses. Clever enemies also target the nature of our rage and our desperation as their most practical weapon in their hands to be used against us. African-Americans know of and remember the strength and courage established for the Algerian determination (revolution for their freedom), for the Libyan determination, and for the Egyptian determination. Egypt's courage was not shamed or defeated in its war with Israel to save Jerusalem and check Israel's aggression towards the Palestinians.

"However, the problem did not yield to Arab national forces. Calling national fervor "Islamic jihad' serves only to make us more despicable before Allah and also more despicable before man (the world).

"Regarding threats from enemies and their cruel designs on the world of Muslims, it is clear what is needed most is improved awareness on one side, an awareness of what is missing in our constitution and in our strengths as Muslims, and an awareness on the other side, an awareness of the vulnerability (the weaknesses) that are in our determined enemies. We need to know the weaknesses in our enemies which expose them (the enemies) to approved Muslim weapons (and I am not talking about physical weapons) making our weapons effective.

"It may not be this simple, but we will agree that our best defense is a defense of taqwa (regardfulness of God in its broadest sense), truth and decent behavior befitting Muslims. We ask Allah for help and strength to see our enemies clearly and to also see ourselves clearly.

"In America and in the West we have a saying (I'm sure as scholars you are familiar with this): 'A hint to the wise is sufficient.' I find that saying very helpful to me in this difficult situation for me as I address you. Without the credits of the scholars and coming from where I do, I want to say 'a hint to the wise is sufficient.' (I wish I had expressed this in fewer words.)"

31   Review and Outlook Opinion-Editorial. "The Caliphate Rises" (The Wall Street Journal, June 28-29, 2014)

"The jihadists of the Islamic State of Iraq and al Sham (ISIS) continue to consolidate their grip on Sunni Iraq. They control most major cities....

"It's important to understand how large a setback for American interests and security this is. Establishing a caliphate in the Middle East was the main political project of Osama bin Laden's life. Current al Qaeda leader Ayman al Zawahiri once said a new caliphate would signal a turning

of world history 'against the empire of the United States and the world's Jewish government.'

"In 2005, a Jordanian journalist named Fouad Hussein wrote a book on al Qaeda's 'second generation,' which focused on the thinking of terrorist Abu Musab al-Zarqawi, who was killed by U.S. forces in 2006. The book described a seven-phase plan, beginning with an 'awakening' of Islamic consciousness with the September 11 attacks. Among other predictions, it foresaw an effort to 'clear plans to partition Syria, Lebanon and Jordan into sectarian statelets to reshape the region.' In phase four, timed to happen between 2010 and 2013, the Arab world's secular regimes would be toppled.

"And then? Phase five would see the 'declaration of the caliphate or Islamic state' sometime between 2013 and 2016. This was to be followed by 'total war,' or the 'beginning of the confrontation between faith and disbelief,' which would begin in earnest after the establishment of the Islamic caliphate."

Author's note: The above-described 'phases' that reflect the 'rise' of extremist interpretations of Islam have a direct correlation to the Persian Gulf War. While it can be argued that political, social, and economic issues bear their mark on the unrest among populations in these states that the extremists feed upon, it cannot be denied that the presence and image of American and other non-Muslim troops in the region lit the fuse for the extremist's response to what they interpreted as a new offensive or 'Crusade' against Islam.

32   Other Western democracies share, with the U.S., concern over the growing influence of extremist Muslim ideologies internationally and within their own states. In a recent speech (April, 2014), the former Prime Minister of the United Kingdom, Tony Blair, identified extremist Muslims as the force "holding back the proper political, social, and economic advance" of the Middle East—and by virtue of the inter-connectivity of nations—all other parts of the world. Further on this subject, he said:

"...There is a titanic struggle going on within the region between those who want the region to embrace the modern

world — politically, socially and economically — and those who instead want to create polities of religious difference and exclusivity. This is the battle. This is the distorting feature. This is what makes intervention so fraught but non-intervention equally so. This is what complicates the process of political evolution. This is what makes it so hard for democracy to take root.

"...It is in fact a struggle in which our own strategic interests are intimately involved... But what is absolutely necessary is that we first liberate ourselves from our own attitude. We have to take sides... We have to have an approach to the region that is coherent and sees it as a whole. And above all, we have to commit. We have to engage.

"... Finally, we have to elevate the issue of religious extremism to the top of the agenda. All over the world the challenge of defeating this ideology requires active and sustained engagement." .

33   In brief, the Islamic principle of 'binding and engagement' (*wa rabitu wa jahidu*) draws upon those concepts and teachings in Islam that obligate 'believers' to construct bonds of trust through relationships with fellow human beings who may abide different religions, philosophical ideas, or political convictions; but share core human values like stability of families and communities, and national security and peace. By 'binding' faith with civic virtue the process fuses seemingly disparate ideas, identities, and peoples through the practice of orthodox Islam, elevating the civic commitments, duties, and loyalties a Muslim citizen owes his fellow citizens and government, Muslim or not, from a secular function to an act of worship. In other words, and in the instance of combating extremist Muslim ideologies as discussed in this book, by serving a nation's legitimate public and common needs, the 'believer' is obeying what his religion asks of him.

The 'engagement' component of this principle builds from the affirmative results of the 'binding' process. It can be focused to either bolster positive forces that sustain essential structures in society, or fight against negative forces that seek to destroy those structures. Within each scenario, the principle's objective is to 'engage' the schemes which threaten the proper function of society with the skilled use of orthodox Islamic teachings cited for their potent affirmation of just causes; or uncompromising refutation of corrupt influences, the worst corruption being injustices meted upon innocents in the name of Islam.

Among the many complex possibilities and advantages this principle offers, its most fundamental use can permanently debilitate the influences of extremist Muslims. With a clear-path operation, it instructs and sensitizes its user in the knowledge and precise methods with which to discredit and nullify extremist ideology using the Qur'an and tradition of Muhammed the Prophet.

Additionally, the principle can be adapted to specifically target, disrupt, and obstruct extremists' recruitment philosophies and techniques. Adding the study of this principle to the training regimen of authorities can provide invaluable intellectual support for developing more effective national security and counter-terrorism initiatives. It can also be utilized as an essential aid where the briefing of Muslim assets is a necessary part of those initiatives.

Part III: The Principle of this book cites the authoritative references from the Qur'an and tradition of Muhammed the Prophet from which 'binding and engagement' is derived. Part three also provides an analysis of how the principle can be effectively applied.

[34] For this discussion, the term 'proto-extremist' refers to the actions, ideas, symbolism, teachings, or principles of Islamic origin that are cited by Muslims to justify, acknowledge, or otherwise legitimize the ideologies and behaviors of extremist Muslims. These Muslims do not participate in extremist behaviors personally, nor materially support extremist causes, but generally sympathize with their premises and logic.

For example, the overwhelming majority of Muslims who refer to themselves as *Salafi* would not fall into the extremist category by their personal beliefs or individual behavior. However, because of their interpretations and emphasis in Islam, a number of Muslims identifying with them could embrace or support extremist behavior. For this reason the *Salafi* 'school' is considered a proto-extremist idea.

[35] Any Muslim, or Muslim-American in particular, who is familiar* with that which is advocated by the Islamic principle

of 'binding and engagement,' are poised for service in dealing extremist Muslim ideologies a fatal blow. The Qur'an says:

> "Those who believe fight in the cause of God and those who reject faith fight in the cause of evil. So fight you against the supporters of Satan: feeble indeed is Satan's scheme." (4:76)

> "Let there arise from you a cooperative of people inviting to all that is good, enjoining what is known to be right and shunning what is wrong...." (3:104)

*Muslims may be generally aware of the Islamic teachings referenced by this principle without being familiar with the principle by name.

Part II: Identity

3 Islamic Memory

[36]   Kidd, Thomas S. "American Christians and Islam: Evangelical Culture and Muslims from the Colonial Period to the Age of Terrorism" (Princeton University Press, 2009, pgs.112-113)

> "One of the key signals of a new domestic Muslim presence in America was the opening of the elaborate Islamic Center in Washington, D.C. in 1957. President Dwight Eisenhower spoke at the dedication of the Center, assuring American Muslims that they were welcome in America because of the nation's commitment to freedom of religion.... The new Muslim community grew slowly in America before 1965, but after immigration reforms of that year many more Muslims began arriving from overseas."

[37]   Gomez, Michael A. "Black Crescent: The Experience and Legacy of African Muslims in the Americas." (Cambridge University Press, 2008, Prologue)

> "In 1492, Christopher Columbus crossed the Atlantic, and with him came Islam. Among his crews were Muslims who had been forced to profess the Christian faith; it is highly probable that Islam remained embedded in their souls. To these and others similarly stationed throughout the western hemisphere in the fifteenth and sixteenth centuries were

*added enslaved Africans, some of whom were also Muslims.
Through the nineteenth century, the numbers of African
Muslims transported to the Americas continued to grow."*

[38]   Author's note: The word 'Islam' is derived from the Arabic
root *s-l-m* which suggests peace, well-being, contentment,
resignation, or submission. The term 'Muslim,' similarly
derived, in its most fundamental usage, describes the nature of
created matter to 'submit' to the parameters and functions of its
own design. In the technical religious sense, a Muslim abides
his Creator's authority by acts of devotion, which, among ritual
practices, ultimately requires establishment of a worshipful
society. The Muslim is a conscientious servant of his Creator,
and therefore a steward for all creation.

The slave's existence, under the American system of slavery,
presented no meaningful opportunity to observe or maintain
the proper practice of Muslim faith. The slave who had been
a Muslim in Africa could only dwell in heart and mind on
his Islamic life, and likewise, could only impart to his family
that which was most memorable and could be concealed from
authorities. Because of the obvious constraints of the slave
system, ritual practices, i.e., daily prayers, Qur'anic study, etc.
would have been virtually impossible; not to mention any type
of Islamic communal observance with fellow 'Muslim' slaves.
With the exception of the Islamic memory, nothing of Islam
could have been sustained in the slave's environment.

[39]   See Gomez, pgs. 159-161

> *"Despite the vitality of the Islamic tradition and the strength
> of their bonds, Muslims [slaves] faced certain distinct
> challenges to the preservation of their faith. Although they
> may have gathered in small numbers and clandestine places
> to pray, they could neither openly maintain Qur'anic schools,
> nor have access to Islamic texts... Allowing for exceptional
> cases... the gradual loss of Islamic knowledge, combined with
> the parochial application of Arabic to religious discourse,
> constituted a blow to the continuation of Islam in the early
> American South....*
>
> *"Enslavement itself introduced structural impediments
> to such matters as formal education, circumcision, the
> formation of brotherhoods, the maintenance of moral*

proscriptions, and the observance of basic dietary rules. The children of African Muslims would have been socialized within the context of the larger, non-Muslim slave culture and deeply influenced by this process. In short, Muslims would have had great difficulty in preserving Islam within their families, assuming a stable, enslaved family."

Author's note: The extraordinary lives of Umar Ibn Said of North Carolina, Ibrahim Abdur-Rahman of Mississippi, Ayyub Sulayman of Maryland and Saalih Bilali of South Carolina have been chronicled in scholarly works (Allan D. Austin's African Muslims in Antebellum America; Sylvia A. Diouf's Servants of Allah: African Muslims Enslaved in the Americas, etc.) as outstanding and exceptional examples reflecting Muslim presence in America during slavery. Their lives are the blessed exception to the rule, leaving us evidence of the Islamic memory.

[40] During the U.S. Constitution ratification debates of 1787, an accommodation was reached by delegates from southern and northern states for tallying a state's total population. For purposes of determining the number of seats a state would have in the House of Representatives and the percentage of tax burden that state would be bear for the nation's debt, it was agreed that a slave would be counted as the equivalent of three-fifths of a human being/citizen.

[41] Sowell, Thomas. "Ethnic America." (Basic Books, 1981, pgs. 197-198)

> *"Although blacks suffered in body and mind under slavery, they did not emerge as a spiritually crushed people. Great numbers of black men fought ably during the Civil War. During the northern occupation of the South, black soldiers controlled and disciplined whites. The position of newly freed blacks was made precarious by the undependable protection of the Union Army and the rampant terrorism used against blacks to try to keep them 'in their place'...."*

[42] Spellberg, Denise A. "Thomas Jefferson's Qur'an: Islam and the Founders" (Vintage Books, 2013, pg.195)

[43] See Gomez, pg. 179

> "[Ibrahim] Abdur-Rahman... and Umar Ibn Said boasted
> of extensive education in West Africa. In fact, it was
> more common than not that West African Muslims were
> recipients of Islamic education and were therefore literate,
> and the various documents that concern notable Muslims
> invariably comment on the fact that they could write in
> Arabic... [I]t should be appreciated that literacy within the
> West African Muslim community was widespread... that the
> educational process was well-established, with a tradition
> reaching back to at least the 14th century."

[44]   Ibid., pg. 161

> "It is therefore with the children and grandchildren of
> African born Muslims that questions concerning the
> resilience of Islam takes on significance. While it cannot be
> established with certainty that the progeny were Muslim,
> the Islamic heritage was certainly there; individuals bore
> Muslim names and retained a keen memory of the religious
> practices of their ancestors."

[45]   Lincoln, Abraham. "The Gettysburg Address." (Excerpts,
November 19, 1863)

> "Fourscore and seven years ago our Fathers brought forth
> on this continent, a new nation, conceived in liberty and
> dedicated to the proposition that all men are created equal.
> Now we are engaged in a great civil war, testing whether
> that nation, or any nation so conceived and so dedicated can
> long endure. We are met on a great battlefield of that war....

> "The world will little note, nor long remember what we say
> here, but it can never forget what they did here. It is for us
> the living, rather, to be dedicated here to the unfinished work
> which they who fought here have thus far so nobly advanced.
> It is rather for us to be here dedicated to the great task
> remaining before us - that from these honored dead we take
> increased devotion to that cause for which they gave the last
> full measure of devotion – that we highly resolve that these
> dead shall not have died in vain – that this nation, under
> God shall have a new birth of freedom, and that government

of the people, by the people, for the people, shall not perish from the earth."

[46]   See Sowell, pg. 197

> *"After two centuries of slavery, in which Negroes were conceived to have no rights, white Southerners resented not only emancipation but also any behavior, words, or attitudes by blacks implying common humanity or common rights. The general attitude of white Southerners toward blacks was aptly summed up by a colonel in the Union Army in the South in 1865: 'to kill a negro they do not deem murder; to debauch a negro woman they do not deem fornication; to take property away from a negro they do not consider robbery.' It was an attitude summarized earlier in the Dred Scott decision, which declared that blacks 'had no rights which the white man was bound to respect.' In short, freedom of American Negroes began in atmosphere that was as uncompromising emotionally as it was economically and politically."*

[47]   See Gomez, pg. 205

> *"[they] may have had some personal contact with Muslims or their descendants, or... had at least some familiarity with concepts associated with Islam...."*

Author's note: Unorthodox, or proto-Islamic organizations like the Moorish Science Temple, Ahmadiyyah Movement, and Nation of Islam began to attract African-American membership in urban centers like New York, Chicago, Detroit, Washington, D.C. and Philadelphia from as early as 1910. It would not be unreasonable to suggest that these organizations developed, in part, as a result of the influence from the Islamic memory of African-American slaves: Drew Ali (Timothy Drew), founder of the Moorish Science Temple was born in North Carolina, and Elijah Muhammad (Elijah Poole), leader of the Nation of Islam was from Georgia. Both were born in the last decade of the 19th century and would likely have had contact with other African-American family and community members who had themselves been born into slavery and could well have retained some memory of an Islamic past.

48   Mohammed, W. Deen. "A Healthy Patriotism." (Speech Excerpts, July, 4, 2004)

> "I am sure Mr. [W.D.] Fard was thinking of our being deprived of liberty. When he came we were discriminated against in the South and treated like unwanted, animal-level people. I am not talking about slavery. I am talking about 1930. The laws weren't changed until about 1960 or after....He saw a people in a country that claimed to be a country of democracy for all, freedom, liberty and justice for all. And he saw that a certain race had been excluded from that and not even recognized as a human being on the level to qualify for that.

> "Mr. Fard said enough in clear and plain language to clear every lie he permitted to be put in his name. And the Founding Fathers [in spite of some being slave-owners] said enough and said it clear enough, that in time it would kill every falsehood or every lie they permitted their names to be put upon.

> "...That is what a true patriot is. He or she lives with something very special and very meaningful as an understanding of what it is to be a citizen of America. They live with that in their minds and in their hearts, and their spirit is drawn to that. And they make sure that their children succeed that... They will make sure that their children understand it and appreciate it.

> "When I began as your leader, I said to myself, 'No way for us to achieve what we want to achieve in this country if we don't do what the rest of the Blacks, especially the civil rights leaders were asking for our people to do.' And that is claim your rights. I said to myself, 'I don't care what they think of me. They may think I am not worthy of the rights and privileges of citizenship. I don't care, as long as I know there is a law that says I should have that.'

> "What you have rights to goes back before the United States – this kind of perception of your entitlement, what you are entitled to as a creature of God on this earth that man did not make. The Creator made it.

"*This goes back to the time before government and even before man and his authority. It is in Islam and in the Qur'an, where the language of the scholars is formed upon the language of the Qur'an.*

"*Every man created is entitled to what God has created. No man is to be discriminated against. It isn't to be based upon anything but justice.*

"*America is saying on this 4th of July that this Nation is built upon the natural evolution of human life. Human life is evolved out of nature, out of the earth by God who planned it. And eventually that life will come to the right perception, the right idea and the right plan for the future of the society.*

"*The Arabs were reading the Qur'an and reading it right about God. We had the Qur'an too, but we were saying 'God was Mr. W.D. Fard in human flesh.' The Arabs knew the Prophet who got the revelation, and they were acknowledging the right Prophet, Muhammed, of Arabia. We were saying that the Honorable Elijah Muhammad was the messenger of God....*

"*But we had good intentions and our religion was sincere. And we wanted to be all the way straight, not part of the way. We were acknowledging God before great America and taking the risk of living our different life here in the face of great America.*

"*Now the same God that I just described sees the poor descendants of slaves, how they were treated and how they wanted to be treated. And He sees in their hearts how they really wanted to be upright and on the right path for God. And they were speaking a language that God couldn't accept.*

"*So God says, 'I'll take care of them. I'll teach them Myself. They are going to learn the Qur'an, and they won't learn it from Arabs. I am going to inspire them, and they are going to learn it from my inspiration. One day I am going to favor them over the rest.'*

"... The Muslims that Allah is with are not those Muslims over there. It is the Muslims in the United States of America, and [we] were here while others were mum and afraid to speak."

4 Injustice, Hypocrisy, and Identity

[49]   Haley, Alex. "Mr. Muhammad Speaks." (Reader's Digest, March, 1960)

> *"As head of a fast-growing, anti-white, anti-Christian cult, this mild looking man is considered 'the most powerful Blackman in America...' His appeal seems to be chiefly among the great masses of Negroes who have migrated to large cities, and have been unable to acquire satisfactory new identities. To these he offers a new way of life...."*

[50]   Muhammad, Elijah. "Message to the Blackman." (Nation of Islam, 1965, pg.38)

> *"Men everywhere are seeking unity among themselves. Every race of people want unity with their own kind first, except my people the so-called Negro in America. Our condition and lack of love for ourselves must be attributed to the slave-master. He has been our teachers until the coming of Almighty God, Allah. The slave-master has robbed my people of their God, religion, name, language, and culture. The worst kind of crime has been committed against us, for we were robbed of our desire to even want to think and do for ourselves."*

[51]   Ibid., pg. 39-40

> *"It is a shame! This shows you and I what white America is to us and just why we have not been able to do anything for self. They want us to be helpless so they can mistreat us always. We must come together and unite. It is time.*
>
> *"I think it is a disgrace for us to be satisfied with only a servant's part. We should and must, as other people, want for ourselves what other civilized nations have! Let us do for ourselves that which we are begging the slave-master*

to do for us. Do not be fooled by the false promise of civil rights and the softening of their language. It is offered to you now to keep you from becoming free of their evil plans of depriving you of the offer made to us by Allah - if we would submit to Him. He will set us in heaven at once. It is only justice that we be given land and provisions for a start so we may do for ourselves....

"Let us make this clear. I am not begging. For, it pleases Allah. He will give us a home, and I am with Him. Today, according to Allah's Word we are living in a time of the great separation of the blacks and the whites....

"Why not Islam? It is our only salvation... Today, God, in the Person of Master Fard Muhammad, is asking you and me to accept our kind and some of this earth, that we call our own...."

52   Muhammad, Elijah. "The Flag of Islam." (Nation of Islam, 1974)

"Master Fard Muhammad... found us, His Black People here in North America which is spiritually referred to as the Wilderness of North America. He has power over the heaven and the Earth. He called us a Nation for the first time. This coincides with the Bible which refers to Him as making a Nation out of us Himself after He found us. Therefore He began at once calling us the Lost Found Nation of Islam in the Wilderness of North America. He brought to us a Flag which represents an independent people....

"Since our Flag has been given to us to represent us as an independent Nation, it is referred to in the words 'The Flag of Islam...' The nature of its science is the greatness of the unlimited wisdom of the Designer, the great source of goodness for all that is under and in the Flag of Islam; the Freedom, the Justice, the Equality that is freely exercised by both believers and non-believers under the Flag of Islam...."

53   See Muhammad., pg.49-50, "Message to the Blackman."

"He has chosen us today to be His people and establish forever a people of righteousness and a people with unlimited

knowledge of the Divine Supreme being. The very last of one of these will become greater than the greatest of this world.

"The Orthodox Muslims will have to bow to the choice of Allah. Allah will bring about a new Islam. As for the Principles of Belief, they remain the same. There will be no more signs to be watched for the coming of God and the setting up of a new world of Islam. We are seeing this change now and entering into it. The devils oppose this change and the Orthodox join them in opposing us because of their desire to carry on the old way of Islam."

pg. 187,

"Many of the Orthodox Muslims do not want to believe that Allah has appeared in the Person of Master Fard Muhammad or that He has made manifest the truth that has been hidden from their religious scientists – the truth of God and of the devil as revealed to me. Though they do have the Holy Qur'an, many of them do not understand the meaning of it...."

pg. 189,

"Some of the well-read scholars among the Orthodox Muslims are grieved to hear from America that I call myself - Messenger of Allah, though not one of them has been able to do the work that I have done in resurrecting my people in America. They could not do it. It was not for them to do what I am doing...."

"... the Holy Qur'an is without doubt a true book, but it only takes us up to the resurrection of the dead not beyond. It does not give you a real knowledge of Allah and the Devil...."

[54]   See Gomez., pg. 310,

"[The Nation of Islam's] most salient concept about the origins of white people is that they are inventions, 'made' (rather than 'created,' a distinction enjoyed only by black folk) by a black man whose own existence, in contrast, was 'natural' and divinely designed. This implies a positional

subjectivity of whites to black folk, the realization of which depends to some extent on the 'mental resurrection' of the previously subjugated. To be more specific, whites are presented as the consequence of an experiment, conducted by a scientist named Yakub or Yacub (both spellings are used in the documents), and they are therefore referred to as 'Yacub's grafted devil.'"

55   Haley, Alex. "The Autobiography of Malcolm X." (Random House Publishing, 1964, pg.171)

> *"I was to learn later that Elijah Muhammad's tales... infuriated the Muslims of the East. While at Mecca, I reminded them that it was their fault, since they themselves hadn't done enough to make real Islam known in the West."*

56   Lewis, Bernard. "What Went Wrong: The Clash Between Islam and Modernity in the Middle East." (Oxford University Press, 2002, pg.89)

> *"[Slavery] remained legal in the Ottoman Empire and in Persia until the early 20th century; it was finally abolished in Yemen and Saudi Arabia in 1962."*

57   King Jr., Martin Luther. "I have a Dream." (Speech Excerpts, August 28, 1963)

> *""Five score years ago, a great American, in whose symbolic shadow we stand today, signed the Emancipation Proclamation. This momentous decree came as a great beacon light of hope to millions of Negro slaves who had been seared in the flames of withering injustice. It came as a daybreak to end the long night of their captivity....*
>
> *"But one hundred years later the Negro is still not free... One hundred years later, the Negro is still languished in the corner of American society and finds himself an exile in his own land. And so we've come here today to dramatize a shameful condition....*
>
> *"When the architects of our republic wrote the magnificent words of the Constitution and the Declaration of*

Independence they were signing a promissory note to which every American was to fall heir. This note was a promise that all men, yes, black men and white men would be guaranteed 'unalienable rights....'

"We refuse to believe that there are insufficient funds in the great vaults of opportunity of this nation. And so we've come to cash this check, a check that will give us upon demand the riches of freedom and the security of justice....

"And so even though we face the difficulties of today and tomorrow, I still have a dream. It is a dream deeply rooted in the American dream.

"I have a dream that one day this nation will rise up and live out the true meaning of its creed: 'We hold these truths to be self-evident, that all men are created equal....'"

[58]   See Qur'an., 3:110,

"You are the best of Peoples, evolved for mankind, enjoining what is right, forbidding what is wrong, and believing in Allah."

[59]   See Muhammad., "Message to the Blackman."

"You must remember that slave-names will keep you a slave in the eyes of the civilized world today. You have seen, and recently, that Africa and Asia will not honor you or give you respect as long as you are called by the white man's name. The example was evident when I took Muhammad Ali (the World's Heavyweight Champion) out of the white man's name (the name itself made him a servant and slave to the white man). All Africa and Asia then acclaimed him as being their champion. This shows you that all of the previous black men of America who were bestowed with the title of world's heavyweight champion were only exalting the white man of America."

[60]   See Haley., pg. 325 "The Autobiography of Malcolm X."

"*[Orthodox Muslims] had said to me that, my white-indicting statements notwithstanding, they felt I was sincere in considering myself a Muslim – and they felt that if I was exposed to what they always called 'true Islam' I would 'understand it and embrace it...' [in] the privacy of my own thoughts after several of these experiences I did question myself: if one was sincere in professing a religion, why should he balk at broadening his knowledge of that religion?*

"*Once in a conversation I broached the subject with Wallace Muhammad, Elijah Muhammad's son. He said that yes, certainly, a Muslim should seek to learn all that he could about Islam. I had always had a high opinion of Wallace Muhammad's opinion.*"

5 The Muslim-American

[61] See Sowell., pg. 286,

"*Acculturation has sometimes been depicted as a one-way process, in which racial and ethnic groups have been forced to surrender their respective cultures and conform... In reality, the American culture is built on the food, the language, the attitudes, and the skills from numerous groups.*"

pg. 296,

"*The history of American ethnic groups, which is to say, ultimately, the history of the American people, is the history of a complex aggregate of complex groups and individuals... It is a story of similar patterns and profound differences of pain and pride and achievement. It is, in one sense, the story of many different heritages. In another sense, it is the story of the human spirit in its many guises.*"

[62] See Spellberg., pg. 278-279,

"*How many American Muslim citizens now reside in the United States? Scholars and pollsters disagree, with estimates ranging from two to eight million... In any case, Islam is the fastest growing religion in the country.*"

[63]   Ibid., Pg. 278,

> "American Muslims represent the most ethnically, racially, and theologically diverse Islamic community in the world. American Muslim citizens hail from seventy-seven countries of origin. Sixty-three percent were born abroad, 37 percent indigenous to the United States... Of the 37 percent indigenous American Muslims, the largest group, 40 percent, are African-American whose families at some point 'reverted' to what they perceived as their original African faith. Many opted for Islam in response to racism and slavery associated with the Christian past. But the ranks of American Muslim converts are racially diverse: 18 percent are white, 10 percent are Asian, 10 percent are Hispanic, and 21 percent claim to be of mixed origin. Hispanic converts, like African-Americans, also identify Islam as their ancestral faith in Spain prior to the fifteenth century. As to varieties of Islam, 65 percent of American Muslims identify as Sunnis, with 11 percent professing Shi'ism and another 24 percent refusing classification as either."

[64]   Al-Hibri, Azizah Y., "Islamic and American Constitutional Law: Borrowing Possibilities or a History of Borrowing?" (University of Pennsylvania Journal of Constitutional Law, I, No. 3, 1999, pg. 504-505)

> "The Qur'an encourages ethnic and other types of diversity as blessings from God. Consequently, ancient Muslim jurists recognized the fact that what may suit one culture may not be quite suitable for another. For this reason, they encouraged each country to introduce its own customs into laws, provided that their customs did not contradict basic Islamic principles... By reserving room for custom, the Law Giver (God) emphasized the importance of cultural diversity and the ability of each society to make its own choices.

> "...the Law Giver recognized both the human ability to constantly evolve and improve and its need to do so over time. For this reason, in an Arab society which at the time of revelation consumed a great deal of wine, the divine prohibition against consuming alcoholic beverages was imposed by the Qur'an gradually. The same feature applied

to the introduction of democracy. Given the pervasive authoritarian ideology in the world at that time (over 1400 years ago), it was clear that human consciousness would need time to recognize the evils of authoritarianism and reject it in favor of democracy. The Qur'an provided the basic principles for a constitutional democracy without providing the details of a specific system. Muslims were to interpret these basic principles in light of their customs and the demands of the historical consciousness, as informed by the era in which they lived."

65   See Qur'an., 9:112,

> *"Those that turn to Allah in repentance; that serve Him, and praise Him; that journey in His Cause, that bow down and prostrate themselves in prayer; that encourage good and eschew evil; and observe the limits set by Allah..."*

66   Ibid., 97:9,

> *"So therefore think! For thinking profits the thinker."*

67   Ibid., 57:21,

> *"Be you foremost in seeking forgiveness from your Lord, and a garden the width whereof is as the width of heavens and earth...."*

Author's Note: Muslim-American thinking interprets this verse to mean that God approves of the freedom of His human creation to pursue his interests within the limits of that which would be considered error and requires forgiveness.

68   "Sahih Al-Bukhari."
69   Author's Note: The formal Islamic prayer, called *salat* is an obligatory act to be performed five times daily (dawn, noon, afternoon, sunset, night) in which precise recitation of the Arabic Qur'an is required.
70   See Qur'an., 39:55,

> *"And follow the best thereof revealed to you from your Lord...."*

See Al-Hibri., pg. 509,

> "Furthermore, no one may oblige another to abide by his or her own understanding of the Qur'an. Since humans are fallible, Muslim jurists recognize the importance of the diversity of opinion and freedom of conscience, even within the same religion. In fact, they view this diversity as a sign of God's mercy, because it allows people to choose that jurisprudence which best suits their condition. For this reason, Muslim schools of thought proliferated, living side by side despite disagreement on important issues."

[71]   See Qur'an., 12:76,

> "We raise the degrees (of knowledge and wisdom) of whom We please: but above all given knowledge is One, the All-Knowing."

[72]   See Bukhari,

> "Narrated on the authority of Abu Huraira, the Prophet said, 'If someone eats or drinks forgetfully while fasting, then his fast is not nullified, and he should complete his fast, for what he has eaten or drunk has been given to him by Allah.'"

Author's Note: The above states an Islamic principle which establishes that to break an ordinance, regulation, or law without malice or harm to self or innocents is not an act of guilt; thus matters are judged by intent, and intent is always presumed good unless shown by irrefutable evidence to be otherwise.

[73]   See Qur'an., 24:64,

> "Be certain that to Allah does belong whatever is in the heavens and on earth. He knows well what you intend; and one day they will be brought back to Him, and He will tell the truth of what they did."

Author's Note: Matters concerning suspicion can potentially plunder the honor of an accused, an accuser, and ultimately the integrity of families, communities, and society at large. Islam emphasizes judgment upon evidence of truth, and presumption of innocence and sincerity above all suspicion.

[74] Author's Note: It is reported in Bukhari that one Muslim observed another performing sincere acts of devotion (prayer, fasting, etc.) but depriving himself and his family of proper attention and care. About this, he advised his brother,

> "Your Lord has a right over you, your own self has a right over you, and your family has a right over you. So you should answer the rights of all who have a legitimate right."

> The story was related to the Prophet to which he said, "[The one who observed] has advised his brother truthfully."

[75] See Qur'an., 49:13,

> "O mankind! We created you from a single pair of a male and a female, and made you into nations and tribes, that you may know each other."

64:3,

> "He... has given you your forms and made them all beautiful."

[76] Ibid., 31:34,

> "...and He knows what is in the wombs. Nor does anyone know what it is that he will earn on the morrow; nor does anyone know in what land he is to die."

[77] Mohammed, W. Deen., "An African-American Genesis." (M.A.C.A. Publication Fund, 1986, pg. 15, 36)

> "If I truly believe in my religion that God has Power over everything, then no matter what the atmosphere or the environment is saying, I'll remember that God is bigger than the environment. He made the environment... He has put in the human being a potential bigger than the challenges of these environments. He has given me a potential equal to the task of the universal environment."

See Qur'an., 14:33,

> "And He has made of service to you the sun and the moon...
> and the Night and the Day He has made of service to you."

4:97,

> "[The angels ask], In what condition were you? They reply:
> 'Weak and oppressed were we in the earth.'
>
> [The angels] say, 'Was not the earth of Allah spacious
> enough for you to move yourselves...?'"

65:2-3,

> "And for those who fear Allah, He ever prepares a way out,
> and He provides for [His creature] from sources he could
> never imagine."

[78]   Ali, Abdullah Yusuf (d. 1952). "The Meaning of the Holy
Qur'an." (Amana Publications, 2011, Preface to the First
Edition, pg. xv)

[79]   See Qur'an., 28:77,

> "But seek with the means you have been given the home of
> the Hereafter but do not neglect your share of this world."

[80]   See Lewis., pg. 79, "What Went Wrong.,"

> "In the medieval Middle East, [Islamic] scientists developed
> an approach rarely used by the ancients - experiment.
> Through this and other means they brought major advances
> in virtually all the sciences.
>
> "Much of this was transmitted to the medieval West ,
> whence eager students went to study in what were then
> Muslim centers of learning in Spain and Sicily, while others
> translated scientific texts from Arabic into Latin, some
> original, some adapted from ancient Greek works. Modern
> science owes an immense debt to these transmitters.

"And then, approximately from the end of the Middle Ages, there was a dramatic change. In Europe, the scientific movement advanced enormously in the era of the Renaissance, the Discoveries, the technological revolution, and the vast changes, both intellectual and material, that preceded, accompanied, and followed them. In the Muslim world, independent inquiry virtually came to an end, and science was for the most part reduced to the veneration of a corpus of approved knowledge."

81   See Qur'an., 2:195,

"And make not your own hands contribute to your destruction, but do good; for Allah loves those who do good."

42:42,

"The blame is only against those who oppress men with wrongdoing and insolently transgress beyond bounds through the land, defying right and justice..."

63:2,

"They make their oaths a screen (for their misdeeds): thus they obstruct (men) from the Path of Allah...."

7:32,

"Say: Who has forbidden the beautiful gifts of Allah which He has produced for His servants, and the things, clean and pure, (which He has provided) for sustenance? Say: They are, in the life of this world and the Day of Judgment, for those who have faith."

82   Excerpts from the last sermon of Prophet Muhammed as reported in the hadith collections of Bukhari and Muslim:

"O people, lend me an attentive ear, for I know not after this year, if I shall ever be amongst you again. Therefore listen to what I am saying to you very carefully and take these words to those who could not be present here today.

"O people, just as you regard this month, this day, and this city as sacred, so regard the life and property of every Muslim as a sacred trust. Return the goods entrusted to you to their rightful owners. Hurt no one so that no one may hurt you. Remember that you will indeed meet your Lord, and that He will indeed reckon your deeds.

"Allah has forbidden you to take usury, therefore all usurious obligations shall henceforth be waived. Your capital, however, is yours to keep. You will inflict nor suffer any inequity....

"O people, it is true that you have certain rights with regard to your women, but they also have rights over you. Remember that you have taken them as your wives only under Allah's trust and with His permission. If they abide by your rights then to them belongs the right to be fed and clothed in kindness. Do treat your women well and be kind for they are your partners and committed helpers....

"All mankind is from Adam and Eve, an Arab has no superiority over a non-Arab, nor a non-Arab has any superiority over an Arab; also a white has no superiority over a black, nor a black has any superiority over a white, except by piety and good behavior....

"Nothing shall be legitimate to a Muslim which belongs to a fellow Muslim unless it was given freely and willingly. Do not therefore do injustice to yourselves....

"Remember, one day you will appear before Allah and answer your deeds. So beware, do not stray from the path of righteousness after I am gone....

"Reason well, therefore O people, and understand the words which I convey to you. I leave behind me two things, the Qur'an and my example, and if you follow these you will never go astray.

"All those who listen to me shall pass on my words to others and those to others again, and may the last ones understand my words better than those who listen to me directly. Be *my witness, O Allah, that I have conveyed your message to your people."*

83   Bulliet, Richard W., "The Case for Islamo-Christian Civilization." (Columbia University Press, 2004, pg. 136)

"A Muslim tradition holds that with every new century there comes a 'renewer' (mujeddid), literally, a person whose mission it is to make Muslim religious life new... The tradition of the renewer testifies to an ingrained Muslim confidence in the capacity of their faith to restore itself after periods of disunity or flagging spirit and to adapt to the challenges that the passage of centuries inevitably brings."

84   Author's Note: Fundamentally, the Muslim-American identity asserts its existence on the ideological foundation that democratic ideals are Islamic, and to abide, promote, and defend them are the responsibility of conscientious Americans and faithful Muslims. It has not been the purpose of this discussion to argue the conviction as much as it has been to state it as a naked truth:

Thomas Jefferson wrote on behalf of a hopeful people in the Declaration of Independence,

"We hold these truths to be self-evident; that all men are created equal and endowed by their Creator with certain unalienable rights - that among these are Life, Liberty, and the Pursuit of Happiness...."

The Holy Qur'an as revealed to Muhammed the Prophet says in 82:6-9:

"O man! What has influenced you to turn from your Lord, the Generous? It is He who created you, and fashioned you in perfect symmetry and proportion, and with inherent demands. His will bears its mark on your (human) form. No, but you reject what is evident!"

85   Author's Note: There is a verse in the Qur'an that is used by Muslims as a supplication of commitment and statement of pledge to the community of faith. It is added here as testimony of Muslim-American devotion to faith and citizenship loyalty:

> "Surely, my prayer, my service of sacrifice, my life and my death are for Allah, the Lord of all the systems of knowledge; no partner has He. This I am commanded and I am of the first to submit." (6:162-163)

Part III: The Principle

6 Security and Peace

[86]   See Qur'an., 31:22,

> "Whoever makes peace with his whole self to God, and is a doer of good, has indeed grasped the most secure hand-hold...."

[87]   Ibid., 59: 23-24,

> "Allah is He, than whom there is no other God – The Sovereign, The Holy One, The Source of Peace, The Guardian of Faith, The Preserver of Safety and Security, The Exalted in Might, The Irresistible, The Supreme: glory to Allah! (High is He) above the partners they attribute to Him. He is Allah, The Creator, The Evolver, The Bestower of Forms. To Him belong the Most Beautiful Names: whatever is in the heavens and on earth, does declare His Praises and Glory: and He is the Exalted in Might, the Wise Judge."

[88]   Ibid., 49:17,

> "They impress on you as a favor that they embraced Islam. Say to them, 'Count not your Islam as a favor upon me: No, Allah has conferred a favor and responsibility upon you....'"

[89]   Ibid., 4:86,

> "When a salutation is offered you, meet it with a salutation more courteous, or (at least) of equal courtesy."

[90]   Ibid., 3:85
[91]   Ibid., 7:181,

> *"Of those We have created are people who have been guided, and thus guide others with truth, thereby establishing justice."*

Author's Note: This verse does not mention any particular tradition of faith, only that "a people" have been guided. The Preamble to the United States Constitution reads in part, "We, the People of the United States, in order to form a more perfect Union, establish justice (and)..., promote the general welfare... do ordain and establish this Constitution...."

[92]   See Spellberg., pg. 133, *"Thomas Jefferson's Qur'an...."*

> *"... Morocco [a Muslim nation] had been the first country to recognize American independence in 1778, but the United States has ignored this overture and failed to send an envoy to establish treaty of peace."*

[93]   The Declaration of Independence
[94]   Preamble to the United States Constitution

7 Extremism's Fiercest Enemy

[95]   Benjamin, Daniel., *"Hatreds Bred by Power Politics."* (Wall Street Journal, June 28-29, 2014, Review)

> *"The Kingdom [Saudi Arabia] poured hundreds of millions of dollars into building mosques and schools, established huge organizations that propagated its puritanical brand of Sunni Islam and flooded the Muslim world with textbooks depicting Shiites as heretics and Christians and Jews as subhuman. The same poisonous springs that nourished the Kingdom's sectarian counterrevolution would later help bring forth al-Qaeda and its offshoots."*

Author's Note: Muslim-Americans have long resisted attempts by Muslims abroad to steer their interpretations of Islam, or otherwise influence their Islamic understanding, allegiances, and thinking. By confidence of their sincerity, devotion, innocence, socialization, and history in America, they maintain a fiercely guarded Islamic autonomy while respecting all decent Muslims and their communities.

See Qur'an., 2:179

> *"In the Law of Settlements there is the preservation of Life,*
> *O you people of understanding, that you may restrain*
> *yourselves."*

[96]   Middle East and Africa., *"The War Against the Islamic State."*
(The Economist, December 13, 2014, pg. 51)

> *"Until the American-led coalition started bombing Islamic*
> *State (IS), the group was focused on spilling the blood of*
> *fellow Muslims and minorities rather than Westerners –*
> *in contrast with al-Qaeda before it. But last August, when*
> *airstrikes began in Iraq, IS started beheading American*
> *and British hostages. And when the bombing extended to*
> *Syria a month later, IS urged devotees to attack Westerners*
> *wherever they were found. A spokesman helpfully suggested*
> *several methods, including poisoning and car accidents."*

[97]   See Qur'an., 16:64,

> *"And We sent down the Book to you for the express purpose*
> *that you should make clear to them those things in which*
> *they differ, and that it should be a guide and a mercy to those*
> *that believe."*

29:69,

> *"And those who strive in Our Cause – We will certainly*
> *guide them to Our Paths. For verily Allah is with those who*
> *do what is right."*

10:32,

> *"And what remains after truth, but error?"*

[98]   Ibid., 2:158,

> *"And if anyone obeys his own demand for good, be sure that*
> *God recognizes and knows it."*

8 Citizenship and Civic Virtue

99   See Lewis., *"What Went Wrong."* Pg.36

100 Author's Note: Often understood as a political term translated as 'nation' or 'state', the Islamic term *ummah* refers specifically to the international, intercultural, interracial fraternity of faith that identifies the Creator of all as the only entity worthy of worship and Muhammed of seventh century Arabia as the Creator's Messenger. The term as defined by the Qur'an is too broad to be representative of a particular regional or continental area; philosophical or ideological base. It is the term which describes Islam's universal appeal and mission.

101 Qutb, Sayyid., *"In the Shade of the Qur'an"* (The Islamic Foundation, Volume 3, pg.286)

> *"Once there is a place on earth, any place, which belongs to Islam and where one can feel secure declaring one's faith and fulfilling one's religious duties, then one must migrate in order to live under the banner of Islam...."*

102 Ibid., Volume 2, pg.732-733,

> *"Nor does Islam tolerate that some hypocrites should be described as believers, simply because they have made the verbal declaration that there is no deity other than God and that Muhammad is His Messenger, but, at the same time, remain in the land of unfaith, giving their support to the Muslim's enemies. Such tolerance is, in fact, not tolerance at all but indulgence."*

103 Author's Note: I am an eye-witness to four specific occasions when the late leader of Muslim-Americans, Imam W. Deen Mohammed, expressed sharply different opinions on the matter of the status of Christians, Jews, and others as perceived by Islam from that of contemporary scholars and leaders in the Muslim world. Each occasion involved a personality of some renown, e.g., Abdul-Aziz bin Baz of Saudi Arabia, Hassan Al-Turabi of Sudan, Anwar Ibrahim of Malaysia, and Prince Muhammad Al-Faisal bin Abdul-Aziz of Saudi Arabia. In each instance he defended the status of the 'People of the Book' and others as believers citing specific Qur'anic evidences and opinions of Muhammed the Prophet. At the conclusion of one such encounter Shaykh bin Baz, who was at the time the highest Islamic authority in Saudi Arabia commented, "We

have been so long in our own understanding we have missed the manifestation of the Prophet's prediction, that the latter ones see better and clearer than us."

[104]   Editorial., *"Terrorism Is At Odds With Islamic Tradition."* (Los Angeles Times, August 22,2001)

> *"Some Islamists today argue that the only effective way of resisting oppression or occupation is through terrorism and, therefore, it has become a necessary evil. But this type of unprincipled and opportunistic logic is not supported by the rigorous classical heritage [in Islam]... Modern Muslim terrorist groups are more rooted in national liberation ideologies... than they are in the Islamic tradition. In short, modern Muslim terrorism is part of the historical legacy of colonialism and not the legacy of Islamic law."*

[105]   See Qur'an., 30:30,

> *"So set your attitude for religion correctly, the (identical) pattern upon which He has made mankind...."*

[106]   It is reported in the authentic collections of Prophet Muhammed's tradition (Bukhari, Muslim) that he said,

> *"Every child is born with the perfect and obedient natural pattern, but his parents can change him."*

[107]   See Qur'an., 29:46,

> *"And do not contend with the People of the Book, except in means that are excellent...."*

[108]   See Part I Note #2
[109]   See Qur'an., 9:118,

> *"... (they felt guilty) to such a degree that the earth seemed constrained to them for all of its spaciousness, and their souls seemed straitened to them...."*

[110]   . Ibid., 18:47,

> "... you will see the earth as a level stretch, and we shall draw them all together, nor will we leave out any one of them."

77:25-26,

> "Have We not made the earth a place to draw together the living and the dead."

111 Ibid., 4:112,

> "He who commits a wrong, and then casts blame on an innocent person, burdens himself with both falsehood and clear wrongdoing."

Author's Note: In the history of Islam during the time of the Prophet there is reported an episode where a Muslim who had stolen a shield from one of the Prophet's companions hid it in the home of a Jewish citizen of Madinah and falsely accused him. The Prophet, once the truth of the matter had been revealed, insisted that the Jewish man be fully exonerated. This was during a time when the Muslim community was engaged in a wider struggle with the Jews of Madinah.

112 See Qur'an., 49:14,

> "[They] say, 'We believe', say, 'You have no faith; but you should only say 'We have submitted our wills to Allah, for faith has not yet entered your hearts.'"

3:67,

> "They said with their mouths that which was not in their hearts."

7:165,

> "And when they forgot that which they had been reminded, We saved those who had forbidden wrongdoing and seized those who committed wrong with a severe punishment because they were defiantly disobeying."

6:144,

"Then who does more wrong than one who invents a lie against Allah, to lead mankind astray without knowledge. Certainly Allah does not guide a wrongdoing people."

2:127,

"And whoever undermines what Allah has ordered to be joined and do mischief on earth: these cause loss only to themselves."

42:42,

"The blame is only against those who oppress men with wrongdoing and insolently transgress beyond the boundaries through the land defying right and justice."

63:1,

"When the hypocrites come to you they say, 'We bear witness that you are indeed the Messenger of Allah.' And Allah knows that you are His Messenger, and Allah witnesses that the hypocrites are indeed liars."

[113] Ibid., 4:58,

"Allah commands that you render back your trusts to those whom they are due. And when you judge between men that you judge with justice...."

23:8,

"[The believers] are those who faithfully fulfill their trusts and covenants."

9 Declaration

[114] See Qur'an., 2:143

"Thus We have made you a community justly balanced that you may be a witness for humanity."

[115] Ibid., 49:7

"God has endeared the faith to you, and made it beautiful in your hearts, and He has made hateful to you the covering of faith, egregious wrongdoing, and insidious defiance (against what is right)...."

[116] Ibid., 34:18

"Between them and the cities on which We had granted blessed (institutions), We also placed cities with (other) institutions and infrastructures easily recognized, and between them fair matriculation (was encouraged). There was security of movement and activity between them night and day."

[117] Ibid., 2:191

"... for oppression is a worse wrong than murder or slaughter...."

[118] Ibid., 17:33

"Nor take any life, which God has made (life) sacred, except for just cause..."

[119] Ibid., 22:60

"And if one has defended himself and responded to no extreme, and then is attacked again for no cause, then God will help him."

[120] Ibid., 3:110

"You are the best community made manifest for the good of humanity...."

[121] Ibid., 33:32

"...speak with words firm and just."

[122] Ibid., 39:18

> *"Those who listen to the word and follow the best meaning in it...."*

[123]   Ibid., 2:193

> *"And fight them until there is no more oppression and wrongdoing and there prevail justice and evidence before God...."*

10 Narrative of Joseph

[124]   See Qur'an., 59:18,

> *"O you have faith! Properly regard God and let every individual contribute to his own future...."*

[125]   Widodo, Joko., "Getting down to business in Indonesia," (Economist., pg. 74, the World in 2015)

[126]   Editorial – Opinion., "The state and Islam: Converting the Preachers." (Economist., pg. 52, December 13-19, 2014)

[127]   See Qur'an., 15:9,

> *"We have without doubt, sent down the Remembrance, and We will certainly protect it from corruption."*

85:21-22,

> *"No doubt, this is a glorious Qur'an in protected pages."*

56:77-78,

> *"That this is indeed a Qur'an most honorable, in a fortified Book."*

5:48,

> *"To you we revealed the Book in truth bearing an affinity to the Book preceding and ensuring its safety...."*

[128]   Author's Note: The most important safeguard of the Qur'an is its memorization in entirety by tens of millions, if not more, of the Muslim faithful. Second only to the memorization is its

recitation for all daily prayers which requires memorization of specific chapters and significant selections from it.

129   See Qur'an., 4:113,

> *"But for the grace of God to you and His mercy a group of them would certainly have plotted to lead you astray. But in fact they will only lead themselves astray and to you they can do no harm in the least. For God has sent down to you the Book and wisdom and taught you what you did not know before."*

17:45,

> *"When you recite the Qur'an, We put between you and those who do not believe in the hereafter an invisible partition."*

130   Ibid., 2:59,

> *"But the extremists changed the word from that which had been given them; So We sent on the extremists a plague from heaven, for that they violated Our command repeatedly."*

2:74,

> *"Then woe to those who write the Book with their own hands, and then say: "This is from God, to traffic with it for a miserable gain! Woe to them for what their hands write and for the gain they make thereby."*

15:91,

> *"...[punishments on those] who have made the Qur'an into shreds."*

42:21,

> *"What! Do they have authorities with law from some religion without God's permission?"*

53:28,

> *"But they have no knowledge therein. They follow nothing but conjecture, and conjecture avails nothing against the truth."*

[131]   Ibid., 6:144,

> *"...but who does more wrong than one who invents a lie against God to lead mankind astray without knowledge."*

38:28,

> *"Shall We treat those who have faith and work good deeds the same who do wrong on earth? Shall we treat those who guard against wrongdoing the same as those who turn toward wrongdoing?"*

[132]   Ibid., 42:52,

> *"...you know not before what the Book was, or what faith was; but We have made the Qur'an a light wherewith We guide our servants as We will – and surely you do guide mankind to the straight way."*

[133]   Ibid., 56:78-79,

> *"In a Book fortified, which none shall touch but those who have purity (of intent)."*

[134]   See Bukhari,

> *"Convey from me, even if it is one verse...And whomever tells a lie on me intentionally, then let him find his seat in hellfire."*

[135]   See Qur'an., 12:3

> *"We do relate to you the most excellent of narratives in that We reveal this part of the Qur'an. Before this, you were among those who did not know it."*

[136]   Ibid., 27:76,

"Verily, this Qur'an explains to the children of Israel most of the matters in which they disagree."

Author's Note :The children of Israel are understood in the science of scriptural study to be the first group in a community identity to be 'guided' with instructions on proper construction of human society. In this way they represent the trials and tribulations of human society. Thus, the Qur'an's teachings are for all who identify in the 'guided' tradition. In other words, the Qur'an intends guidance for any society which wants to employ what is in its best interests.

137 Ibid., 12:7,

"Surely, in Joseph and his brothers are messages for those who inquire."

138 Ibid., 12:52,

"...the human individual is subject to fall under influences."

139 Ibid., 12:9,

"Kill Joseph or cast him out to some land that so the favor of your father may be given to you alone. There will be time to be righteous after that."

12:33,

"... Unless you turn their scheme away from me I may feel inclined toward them and join the ranks...."

Author's Note: The argument for destruction of society is that something better is to replace it. The anarchists argument is that the "ends justify the means." An evil thing can be done in the short-term for a good thing to be established in the long. Such arguments are very attractive, but they plunder and pillage innocent lives and structures thus making them Islamically unacceptable.

140 Ibid., 12:20,

"...in such low estimation did they hold him."

[141]   Ibid., 12:8,

> "They said, 'Truly Joseph and his brother are loved more by
> our father than we: but we are a special group....'"

[142]   Ibid., 12:13,

> "I fear the wolf will devour him while you are oblivious...."

12:48,

> "Then will come after that an awful seven which will
> annihilate what you value...."

[143]   Ibid., 12:49,

> "Then will come after that a year in which the people will
> have abundant water...."

[144]   Ibid., 12:34,

> "So his Lord hearkened to him and turned their scheme away
> from him...."

12:37,

> "...Before any food comes to feed either of you I will surely
> reveal to you the truth and meaning of this before it affects
> you. That is of the duty which my Lord has taught me."

12:24,

> "...but that he saw plainly and clearly evidence from his Lord
> that We might turn him away from evil and shameful deeds."

[145]   Ibid., 12:76,

> "He could not take his brother by the law of the king...."

[146]   Ibid., 12:29,

> "O Joseph, excuse this!"

12:93,

> *"Go with my shirt and cast it over the face of my father, he will come to see clearly then come to me together with all of your family."*

Author's Note: Common kindness, general courtesy, cultural traditions, family ties are all profound and powerful platforms of appeal to thwart schemes against society.

[147]   Ibid., 12:62,

> *"And Joseph told his servants to put their stock in trade into their saddlebags, so they should recognize it only when they returned to their people, in order that they might come back."*

12:70,

> *"…He put the drinking cup into his brother's saddlebag…."*

[148]   Ibid., 12:5,

> *"Do not tell your brothers what you saw…."*

12:58,

> *"They entered his presence, and he knew them, but they did not know him."*

12:77,

> *"…these things Joseph kept locked in his heart, not revealing secrets to them."*

[149]   Ibid., 12:33,

> *"He said, O my Lord, the prison is more suitable than the scheme to which they invite me."*

[150]   Ibid., 12:111,

> "There is, in their stories, instruction for those who think deeply. It is not a false tale…."

[151]   Ibid., 12:59,

> "And when he had furnished them with provisions that satisfied them, he said, bring to me a brother you have from the same father as yourselves. You do witness that I compensate you and provide you support."

[152]   Ibid., 12:92,

> "He said, this day let no blame hang over you…."

[153]   Ibid., 12:2,

> "We have sent it down as an Arabic Qur'an, in order that you may work with its logic."

[154]   Ibid., 39:23,

> "God has revealed the most beautiful message as a Book, consistent with itself but repeating and refining its teachings."

[155]   Ibid., 12:77

> "…these things Joseph kept locked in his heart, not revealing secrets to them."

66:3

> "When the Prophet disclosed a matter in confidence to one of his wives…."

71:9

> "Further I have spoken to them publicly and secretly in private."

86:9

> *"the day that all things secret shall be tested"*

[156]   Ibid., 13:10,

> *"It is the same to Him whether any of you conceal his speech or declare it openly; whether he hides by night or walk freely by day."*

67:13,

> *"And whether you hide your word or publish it, He certainly has full knowledge of the secrets of all hearts."*

[157]   See note #151

Part IV: Focus

11 Dismantling Extremist Doctrine

[158]   Al-Ghannushi, Rashid., "Participation in Non-Islamic Government." (Oxford University Press, 1998, pg. 92)

> *"A just government, even if not Islamic, is considered very close to the Islamic one, because justice is the most important feature of an Islamic government, and it has been said that justice is the law of God."*

> Ramadan, Tariq., "To be a European Muslim." (Leicester, UK, Islamic Foundation, 1999, pg.22)

> *"...to defend justice cannot be to defend Muslims only: the best witness of the excellence of the Islamic way of life lies in respecting the ideal of justice over and above the failings of Muslim believers."*

[159]   See Qur'an., 60:7,

> *"It may be that God will grant love and friendship between you and those whom you now hold as enemies. For God has power over all things...."*

59:14,

> *"You think they were united but their hearts are divided because they are a group that do not understand."*

[160]   See Bukhari.,

> *"Islam is 'constructed' upon five essentials...."*

> *"The Prophets were 'constructing' a structure. I am its final brick."*

[161]   See Qur'an., 2:179

[162]   See Note 58

Selected References

THE HOLY QUR'AN
(Author's Note: The overwhelming majority of citations made in this book are from the Holy Qur'an. In its original Arabic it is understood by Muslims to be the eternal, uncorrupted word of God revealed to Muhammed the Prophet for the benefit of humanity. It is the primary source of guidance for the Muslim faithful and the foundation for all knowledge and structures of Islamic society. Comprehension of it, as well as its preservation and utility for humanity, is of the highest and most sacred importance to Muslims. Its perfect recitation is a requirement for ritual worship, and tens of millions worldwide have committed it to memory in its entirety. The quotations used in this book combine both literal and interpretive English translations, as it is impossible to capture the full meanings of the original in any other language but its own Arabic. These translations are drawn from understandings most widely accepted by learned English-speaking Muslims and my own training in its meanings.)

SAHIH AL-BUKHARI
SAHIH MUSLIM

(Author's Note: These are the hadith or narrations of
Muhammed the Prophet's sayings, teachings, actions,
and traditions as collected from his immediate family
members, closest companions, and most trusted
and erudite followers from the first few successive
generations after his passing. The science of hadith is
as inexact as it is strict, with reports on the Prophet's
life ranging from sources who have a nearly irrefutable
status to those which are highly questionable. Thus,
several collections of hadith exist. However, the two
referenced here are graded by Islamic scholars to be of
the highest and most sound authenticity. In conjunction
with the Holy Qur'an these collections rank as a primary
source of Islamic knowledge and guidance.)

PERIODICALS

Reader's Digest
The Economist
The Los Angeles Times
The New York Times
The Wall Street Journal
The Washington Post

BOOKS

An African-American Genesis (W. Deen Mohammed,
MACA Publications, 1986)
Black Crescent: The Experience and Legacy of African
Muslims in the Americas (Michael Gomez, Cambridge
University Press, 2008)
Collection of Religious Rulings (Ahmed Ibn
Taymiyyah, d.1283)
Ethnic America (Thomas Sowell, Basic Books, 1981)
In the Shade of the Qur'an (Sayyid Qutb, 1963)
Message to the Blackman (Elijah Muhammad, 1965)

The Autobiography of Malcolm X (Alex Haley, Random House Publishing, 1964)

The Case for Islamo-Christian Civilization (Richard W. Bulliet, Columbia University Press, 2004)

Thomas Jefferson's Qur'an (Denise A. Spellberg, Vintage Books, 2013)

To Be A European Muslim (Tariq Ramadan, Islamic Foundation, 1999)

What Went Wrong: The Clash Between Islam and Modernity in the Middle East (Bernard Lewis, Oxford University Press, 2002)

In Memoriam

"If we are to succeed in defeating terrorism we must enlist Muslim communities as some of our strongest allies. Muslim leaders here have to continue working with us to decisively and unequivocally reject the hateful ideology that extremist groups promote, and to speak out against not just acts of violence but also those interpretations of Islam that are incompatible with the values of religious tolerance, mutual respect, and human dignity. "

Barack Obama,
President of the United States,
December 6, 2015

In memory of the innocent victims the world over whose lives have been lost to the illicit weaponization of misguided and manipulated convictions: Their lives call out collectively to an international, inter-racial, inter-ethnic, inter-community, interfaith human conscience. We must hear, see, and promote the sanctity of homes, the dignity of peoples and their struggles, and the blessedness of free choices. Within this recognition there is a just order and enduring peace for humanity and nations.

God says in the Qur'an: "It is no inherent fault in the blind, nor in one with a disability, nor in one with a disorder, nor in yourselves - that you should eat in your own homes, or those of your fathers, your mothers, your sisters, your father's brothers, your father's sisters, your mother's brothers or your mother's sisters, or in homes which the keys are in your possession, or in the house of your true friend; there is no cause to blame if you eat with company or separately. But if you enter each other's homes salute each other in peace - as in recognized greeting, or a blessing with purity from God. Thus does God make clear the signs to you that you may understand."

-The Author

Index

Author's Note: This index identifies technical terms and language, historical personages or important individuals, and geographical locations which represent or in some way touch upon the consistent themes of this book. It does not include entries for 'Islam', 'Holy Qur'an', 'Muhammed the Prophet', 'Muslim', 'Muslim-American', or 'extremism,' as these are central to our discussion, and are therefore ubiquitous in this book. Terms of Arabic or Islamic origin that may be unfamiliar to the general reader include a brief explanatory note as to their use. Also, proper names of Arabic or Islamic origin may have various English renderings, as with the multiple spellings of the name 'Muhammed' i.e., Muhammad and Mohammed. Their use herein intend respect for traditional Islamic teachings and sensitivities, and historical accuracy.

CPSIA information can be obtained
at www.ICGtesting.com
Printed in the USA
LVOW10s0224180817
545478LV00021B/786/P

9 781495 809538